Light and Life, environmental ethics is not concerned with the avoidance of death, but with the celebration of life."

Udo W. Middelmann
president, The Francis A. Schaeffer Foundation

"*True North* raises the bar and provides a whole new standard on how to address creation care. It is biblically faithful and theologically rich. It will, I believe, become a classic in the field."

Daniel L. Akin
president, Southeastern Baptist Theological Seminary, Wake Forest, North Carolina

"Liederbach and Bible do an excellent job of putting the whole creation care debate into a solidly biblical and Christocentric context. Their book is clearly written, exegetically sound, and governed by a creation-fall-redemption worldview animated by a passion for Jesus Christ and his kingdom. I recommend it to everyone who longs to transcend the polarization of the debate and to step back from the technical arguments in order to gain a measure of balanced biblical wisdom that is also theologically and philosophically sophisticated."

Al Wolters
professor of religion and theology/classical languages, Redeemer University College, Ancaster, Ontario, Canada
author, *Creation Regained*

"We have desperately needed a biblical theology to orient the complex discussions of creation care. That is what Liederbach and Bible have given us in *True North*. With a solid worldview basis, the discussions can be directed by God's own truth rather than using biblical passages as launching pads for ideas. Those looking for an entry point to the discussions will do well to start with the helpful and biblical introductions to issues and people in *True North*."

Gerry Breshears, Ph.D.
professor of theology, Western Seminary, Portland, Oregon

"*True North* moves the discussion of creation care to its ultimate reason: an act of worship that flows from the essence of our Christian being as we direct our focus *true north* to our Lord. Liederbach and Bible write from their theological/ethical roots as they lay a strong Christological argument for creation care that calls Christians to move past proximate motives of environmental crisis and shallow stewardship to a full life of worship within the grand scope of creation. *True North* is written in a style that is easily accessible to the lay person as well as the scholar. Its both/and discussion of creation care and the Great Commission as essential components of the Christian life is refreshing to hear in a world where either/or arguments often dominate. Indeed, the case is made that all efforts at environmental stewardship are on a shallow foundation without a personal grounding in Christ as Lord."

Dr. Joseph K. Sheldon, Ph.D.
retired distinguished professor of biology and environmental science, Messiah College, Mechanicsburg, Pennsylvania
vice chair of the Board for Pacific Rim Institute for Environmental Stewardship
author, *Rediscovery of Creation: A Bibliographical Study of the Church's Response to the Environmental Crisis*
coauthor, *Redeeming Creation: The Biblical Basis for Environmental Stewardship*

"*True North* is a significant contribution to our understanding of the importance of environmental stewardship. Through careful exegesis of the principal biblical texts, the authors rightly situate the Christian obligation to care for creation as an act of worship of the God of creation. Their approachable yet scholarly reasoning makes this an invaluable guide for the scholar and the layman alike. Their discussion of the shape of Christian ethics toward the end of their volume is a must-read in itself for anyone wrestling with the question of Christian moral behavior."

Barrett Duke, Ph.D.
vice president for public policy and research
director of the research institute of The Ethics and Religious Liberty Commission (ERLC)

"The evangelical creation care movement, and its opponents, need the theological heft that these authors point to. Too many young Christians become enlivened to our stewardship mandate and wind up becoming handmaidens to a secular environmental movement, for lack of deep teaching and rigorous exegesis of Scripture. Too many from an older generation resist environmental responsibilities, also for lack of deep teaching and rigorous exegesis. By anchoring this conversation in a solid Christological context, Liederbach and Bible remind readers that despite the back-and-forth nature of the environmental sound bites offered by the culture, the task of caring for creation is an appropriate part (but not the whole) of following Jesus. They resist the rampant proof texting that afflicts both sides of the current "debate" and instead develop the theological apparatus that supports a considered creation care ethic. They challenge the recent development of environmental ideas with the timeless truths of God's special revelation, and they constantly remind us that Christians can have something fresh and vital to bring to the world's environmental discourse."

Rusty Pritchard, Ph.D.
president and cofounder, *Flourish* ("Reviving lives and landscapes")

"*True North* has the makings of a true classic. It delves further than anything I've seen into the biblical text and context to examine humanity's proper role in God's marvelous creation. The result: a wonderfully rich portrait of mankind helping all creation glorify Christ the Creator. *True North* puts into words A Rocha's underlying ethos and will no doubt help guide our efforts to mobilize Christians to care for creation."

Thomas D. Rowley, LEED AP
executive director, A Rocha USA

"*True North* presents a well-modulated and balanced case for environmental ethics building a solid theological foundation for a Christian understanding of and involvement in creation care. This work uniquely positions Christ, and not crisis, as the center and circumference of creation care. Starting with creation and concluding with the Second Coming, the authors carefully lay out their theological case situating responsible stewardship of creation within a total Christian worldview. This earns *True North* a significant place in the ongoing discussion."

Bruce A. Little, Ph.D.
director, L. Russ Bush Center for Faith and Culture
president of Forum for Christian Thought
professor of philosophy, Southeastern Baptist Theological Seminary, Wake Forest, North Carolina

"This is a book about creation care that even skeptical evangelicals can be excited about. The thinking is fair, biblical, and matured. It is not reactive, as are so many other Christian books on the subject, but puts forward an agenda that begins with the Bible while aware of the cultural narrative. Mark and Seth demonstrate how we can speak with clarity and balance on a subject plagued by extremism and ignorance. To use their metaphor, they give us a compass by which we can navigate the complex and over-rhetoricized issues of environmental care."

J. D. Greear
author, *Gospel: Recovering the Power That Made Christianity Revolutionary*
senior pastor, The Summit Church, Durham, North Carolina

"*True North* is the single best one-stop treatment of creation care from a Christian perspective. Liederbach and Bible trace the biblical narrative from creation and fall through to redemption and restoration, recognizing Christ as the towering Actor in each of those movements, and applying his lordship to the issue of creation care. Those students of theology, ethics, and the environment who neglect this book will do so to their own detriment. Those who read it slowly, carefully, and thoughtfully will reap rich benefits from doing so."

Bruce Ashford, Ph.D.
dean, The College at Southeastern, Southeastern Baptist Theological Seminary, Wake Forest, North Carolina
research fellow, L. Russ Bush Center for Faith and Culture
associate professor of philosophy and intercultural studies

"Liederbach and Bible, two seminary scholars, skillfully weave an apologetic that keeps the focus of creation centered first and foremost on God and Christ. . . . As a Christian, this book is a refreshing approach that profoundly addresses the purpose of creation from a strongly supported biblical perspective. As an ecologist, naturalist, and professor, for me the book clearly links one's thoughts about the creation with an undeniable purpose that allows the reader to understand there is more to creation than random chance and events—there is purpose. This book will be a reference for my research and classroom for a long time to come."

Reginal M. Harrell, Ph.D.
professor of fisheries and wildlife sciences
Department of Environmental Science and Technology
University of Maryland

"*True North* provides the theological insight to the creation care debate that has been lacking in many other works. Beginning with the creation narrative of Genesis and stretching through a consideration of the preeminence of Christ in all things, Liederbach and Bible consistently point their readers back to Scripture and the theological discussions that must be present for a healthy, evangelical conversation about environmental issues. While readers will not walk away with a to-do list for addressing environmental concerns, they will be enamored with the magnificence of Christ as Creator, Redeemer, and King. Above all, Liederbach and Bible provide a model for how to approach any ethical issue with Scripture being the foundation."

Evan Lenow, Ph.D.
assistant professor of ethicsassociate director of the Land Center for Cultural Engagement
Southwestern Baptist Theological Seminary, Fort Worth, Texas

"I commend *True North* by Mark Liederbach and Seth Bible as much for the character of its authors as for its content. This book addresses one of the most challenging areas of moral debate in our culture today, and readers will find its content highly relevant, timely, and accessible. But I can attest, from personal experience, that the moral fiber and spiritual wisdom of the book's authors say more of its reliability and value than mere words can convey. Scholarly writing is a fine thing. But writing by scholars out of hearts aligned to worshipping the One True and Living God is altogether better."

The Hon Revd Dr Daniel R. Heimbach
senior professor of Christian ethics, Southeastern Baptist Theological Seminary
research institute fellow, SBC Ethics and Religious Liberty Commission
editor, B&H Christian Ethics Series
chairman, ETS Christian Ethics Section

"*True North* makes the audacious claim that Jesus holds the keys of truth and knowledge about how we should live upon this earth that God has created and given to us for responsible, appreciative, and loving nurture. The authors constantly emphasize that creation (and most prominently, humans as sentient creatures) has its purpose in worship of God, that is, to magnify the glory of God. To quote, 'The created order has within it an inherent or intrinsic goodness apart from its instrumental value that it plays in the life and existence of human beings.' This book shows Christians how to view the earth we live upon through the Jesus whom we claim as Lord."

Allen Johnson
Christians for the Mountains

"The single most important question that must be asked and answered in our day is this: 'What is truth?' Nowhere is this more needed than in the latter-day controversy over so-called creation care. With impeccable reasoning, anchored in a biblically faithful framework, Mark Liederbach and Seth Bible hold the arguments of creation care advocates up against the 'straight stick of truth.' The result? Much needed illumination, clarity, and insight."

Frank Wright, Ph.D.
president and CEO, National Religious Broadcasters

"This is a much-needed book and a must read for the biblically minded person. It does not answer all of the questions Christians are asking about the environment, but it answers the right ones. Liederbach and Bible motivate us to find our 'True North,' and once found, we are able to respond to Christ in worship as we responsibly and joyfully steward his physical creation. I was challenged to rethink some interpretive assumptions I had made in the past concerning creation and convinced that I want to love and care for the things that God loves and cares for now and into eternity."

Dwayne Milioni
associate editor, *Theoecology Journal*
pastor, Open Door Baptist Church, Raleigh, North Carolina

"Liederbach and Bible bring three important strengths to their work. *First*, this is one of the surprisingly few Christian efforts to address environmental issues that begins with the theological foundations. Most of the literature simply cites a few Bible verses (and almost always the few) and then launches into policy discussions. By rooting their analysis in a larger theological understanding, Liederbach and Bible avoid the problem that many efforts to address environmental issues from a religious perspective fall into: ending up with a discussion that ultimately reduces to what can, with only slight exaggeration, be characterized as a question of whether Christ favors amending the Endangered Species Act or not.

"*Second*, Liederbach and Bible draw on their theological training to bring genuine insight to interpretation of passages such as Genesis 1:26–27. Their interpretation is a delight to read after suffering through so many trite interpretations unguided by any knowledge of Hebrew or effort to read the passage within the larger context of Genesis or the Gospels. The authors are too kind to excerpt and criticize the legions of bad interpretations of this passage (and others), but this is a major contribution that is a welcome corrective. Particularly for readers like myself who lack the extensive theological toolkit possessed by Liederbach and Bible, this is a vital contribution.

"*Third*, *True North* provides an important defense of thinking about the environment from both the pantheism of many environmental writers and the almost willful determination by some Christian writers to address the obligation for care of God's creation as imposing real responsibilities on man. The authors successfully navigate a path between naïve environmentalism and cynical acceptance of environmental degradation to provide useful guidance to Christians wondering how to understand their relationship to creation."

Andrew Morris
H. Ross & Helen Workman Professor of Law & Business
University of Illinois at Urbana-Champaign

"Mark Liederbach and Seth Bible attempt to lay out a path for religious leaders concerned with environmental protection consistent with sound spiritual beliefs. The result is a call for stewardship based upon first principles. Many religious leaders share the view that the environment must be preserved, maintained, and improved. As they lend their moral authority to the cause, they will do well to consider the message in *True North*."

Pete Geddes
executive vice president, Foundation for Research on Economics and the Environment

"Many enter the creation care debate with good intentions but little theological or Scriptural bearings. *True North* seeks to remedy this by placing worship of God front and center in the discussion. Guided by the conviction that all things are created *by* God and *for* God (Col 1:17), Liederbach and Bible connect the dots between a posture of Christian worship and environmental ethics. Particularly insightful is their exploration of key verses in Genesis and the implications for relating to creation."

Ryan Messmore
William E. Simon Fellow in Religion and a Free Society, The Heritage Foundation

TRUE
NORTH

David,

appreciate all your Service
to Christ & Partnership in
the Gospel

Mark Liederbach

1 Cor. 10:31

TRUE NORTH

Christ,
the Gospel,
and
Creation Care

MARK LIEDERBACH
and SETH BIBLE

ACADEMIC
Nashville, Tennessee

ISBN: 978-1-4336-7688-8

Published by B&H Publishing Group
Nashville, Tennessee

Dewey Decimal Classification: 231.7
Subject Heading: CHRIST \ CREATIONISM \ CONSERVATION OF
NATURAL RESOURCES

Unless noted otherwise, Scripture quotations are from the New American
Standard Bible. ©The Lockman Foundation, 1960, 1962, 1968, 1971, 1973,
1975, 1977. Used by permission.

Scripture quotations marked HCSB are taken from the Holman Christian
Standard Bible ® Copyright © 1999, 2000, 2002, 2003, 2009 by Holman
Bible Publishers. Used by permission.

Scripture quotations marked NIV are taken from THE HOLY BIBLE, NEW
INTERNATIONAL VERSION®, NIV® Copyright © 1973, 1978, 1984, 2011
by Biblica, Inc.™ Used by permission. All rights reserved worldwide.

Printed in the United States of America

1 2 3 4 5 6 7 8 9 10 • 17 16 15 14 13 12

VP

Contents

To my dearest friend and brother John Liederbach:

Broken by a broken world, you now taste what I most deeply long for.
I am waiting in joyful hope to see you and our
Savior together . . . flourishing.
Shalom, my brother, shalom.

Acknowledgments

W e owe a tremendous debt of gratitude to several of our dear friends who helped us with this manuscript: Adam York, Rocky Wright, Jared Ownby, and Graham Michael. Guys, we couldn't have done it without you!

Also we are thankful for the careful, watchful, and interactive eyes of the elders at North Wake Church: Larry Trotter, Rob Craig, Jeff Doyle, Sam Williams, Stuart Bulman, Greg Matthias, and Tom Iverson. You are friends and co-laborers as well as the guys who know me best and love me anyway. I cannot thank you men enough for the way you shepherd, live out the gospel, and call me up to be a better man!

We are also grateful to Jim Baird and Chris Cowan at B&H, not only for the opportunity, but also for being patient with us during a very demanding season. Thank you!

A special thanks to John Baden (FREE) and Rusty Pritchard (*Flourish*) for graciously providing contexts for us to learn and grow.

Both of us love where we work and are convinced that Southeastern Baptist Theological Seminary is the best seminary on the planet. Each day is a privilege. The men and women we work with make it a joy. Special thanks to Daniel Heimbach, David Jones, Bruce Little, Danny Akin, Dennis Darville, Ken Keathley, Ryan Hutchinson, and Bruce Ashford.

Harriette, the journey gets better every day. Of all the wonders of God's creation, I (Mark) am most thankful for you, my love. Daniel, Hannah, and Katherine: Jesus loves you, and I love you too!

Kristy, in a busy season of life, thank you for your steadfast love and devotion to our marriage and our family. I (Seth) love you far more than I ever thought possible. To my kids—Chloe, Laney, and Tate—one of God's richest blessings on my life is being your dad.

Our deepest thanks to you, our God and Father, unto whom our efforts are always severely lacking even when we are at our best. We are deeply indebted to grace and eternally thankful for mercy. Forgive our short-comings, we pray, and may you find pleasure in our childish attempts to please our Father.

Introduction

I. Our Purposes in Writing This Book

This book is largely born out of two conferences we were blessed to attend relating to the environment and creation care. The first was an *Environmental Stewardship Conference for Religious Leaders*. This incredibly helpful event, which was run with precision and expertise by FREE (Foundation for Research on Ethics and the Environment), not only provided a context in which to learn and interact with great minds representing various religious and political perspectives, it also provided an invaluable foundational knowledge relating to the political and economic dimensions, of environmental policy reform. As we enjoyed the lectures and discussion both of us became increasingly aware of how much richer the interaction would be if the fundamental principles of Christian ethics were understood and played a fundamental role in the conversation. We believe that is a part of our unique training that we humbly hope to interject into the larger discussion on the environment.

The second conference was *Flourish*—a national pastor's conference on the environment. Once again a very helpful and inspirational time for us, this conference was geared particularly for an evangelical audience and was especially helpful for us in discovering how other evangelicals are thinking on the issue. We not only had helpful interactions on issues related to the environment, the conference went a long way in demonstrating both the important role local churches and religious leaders can play in caring for God's world as well as providing helpful direction on how to actually be involved at the local level. While a very positive experience, our time at *Flourish* also allowed us to be in a place to discern where some of the deficiencies lie among the fledgling evangelical arm of the environmental movement. Of importance for this book, three convictions grew in us as we listened, met with other leaders, and gave our presentation during this conference.

First, we were surprised with regard to the manner and use of the Bible in the presentations and discussions. With the exception of a few very solid presentations, both of us were struck at how little of a role an expository presentation of Scripture played in many of the talks and presentations offered. This perspective of ours should not be misconstrued to mean that a strong biblical element was missing. Biblical *themes* where present everywhere (and we know for certain that the organizers greatly desired this element to drive the conference). However, many of the talks and discussions either used Scripture only as a starting point or launching pad, or they almost exclusively interpreted the Scripture via a narrative hermeneutic emphasizing our place in God's story, but not so much how God's Word provides objective criteria for life and practice. Further, among the attendees, it was interesting how few carried and interacted with their Bibles during the event. Even during our own presentation in which we specifically asked participants to interact with us over the Genesis 1 and 2 creation passages, only a fraction of the attendees were able to do so. Thus, in evaluating presentations and discussion interactions, we concluded that if this event was in any way indicative of the movement of evangelicals as a whole, then it would seem that the role of Scripture as the determinate standard of truth and foundational driving point of discussion among the movement as a whole is surprisingly lacking.

A second conviction that took root in us during our time at *Flourish* related to the fact that while there was a lot of talk about God, his creation, and the importance of caring for the environment he created, there was far less theological rigor related to the nature of God and the person and work of Christ than expected. Once again, this should not be misconstrued as our saying that such conversations and ideas were not present; they were. Rather, they seemed to be assumed or taken for granted, and somehow ended up not being central and driving factors in many of the presentations. It then dawned on us that perhaps one of the reasons environmentalism and creation care is having so much trouble getting traction among conservative evangelicals is the lack of explicit and centralized theological rigor in the discussions. Thus, we have a growing conviction that the way this movement will come out of the fringes and enjoy a place of greater concern and acceptance will be through a thorough grounding in, and explicit connection with, a vigorous historically orthodox theology. We have become convinced that the debate about environmental ethics is at its core a debate about the supremacy of Christ in our lives and our community—as is every aspect of Christian ethics. Thus, the central piece of the discussion must be centered on the triune God, with a specific focus on Christ instead of human interests or even the state of this planet we call home. Our worship of him and expansion of his kingdom and glory throughout the earth must be the pre-eminent point of focus.

A third conviction that is directly related to the previous two has to do with the vitally important link that exists between ethics and evangelism and thus, in this context, the link between environmental ethics and evangelism. This conference merely solidified what we have known to be true about the way evangelicals connect—or better stated—do not connect moral concern with specific and direct discussions about salvation through Jesus Christ. Once again we were surprised that at a conference for "evangelicals" there was much talk about social justice (which we applaud), but almost without exception, there was no direct connection made between how emphasizing creation care and environmental concern directly relates to—and can facilitate—evangelism and reaching the lost with the exclusive claims of Christ and the gospel.

We write, then, from these observations and points of conviction. Neither of us claims to be an expert in science, economics, or politics. But we *are* biblical theologians trained in the field of philosophical and Christian ethics. It is from this perspective, then, that we hope to generate discussion and theological engagement regarding the development of a Christ-centered (and therefore gospel-centered) ethic of worship that specifically addresses the issue of creation care and the environment.

Toward that end, this book has two central purposes. First, our goal is to model grounding an evangelical concern for creation care in a commitment to the infallible and inerrant Scriptures, historical and orthodox doctrine, and biblically informed reasoning as the primary sources of authority.

Second, it is also our hope to construct a framework by which believers can productively engage and interact with the environmental ethics discussion from a distinctively Christian point of view. In particular, we will work hard to demonstrate that the whole discussion of ethics (and in this context, environmental ethics) is ultimately a discussion about the supremacy of Jesus Christ over the entire created order, the corporate body of Christ, and the lives of every individual Christian.

Because these are our stated purposes, we believe it is also wise to point out that this book will, therefore, *not* seek to specify particular political agendas, economic policies, or even specific points of social and/or environmental action. Rather, we are attempting to follow the old adage, "If you want a man to eat, give him a fish; if you want him to eat for a life time, teach him how to fish." It is our prayer that we carry out this task in a manner that will please our Lord.

Our methodology, then, is to engage the Scriptures from the point of view of committed belief to their inerrancy and infallibility and to explore the theological ramifications of the Scripture's teaching from a historically orthodox point of view. Ultimately, because all questions of Christian doctrine and practice intersect critically with Christology, we have chosen to limit our discussion in this book to an exploration of Christ as Creator, Redeemer, and Returning King. From this perspective, the question before us is: "What scriptural and theological doctrines, principles, norms, and rules should instruct us on how to be the kind of people (individually and corporately) who will maximally display the glory of God in the way we steward the resources God has entrusted to us?"

How do these convictions relate specifically to the field of environmental ethics, the concern for creation care, and the purposes of this book? The answer to this question provides the third purpose for our writing. We aim to illustrate how the biblical and theological teachings about the person of Christ ought to serve as our moral compass and lead us to the proper expressions of a life of worshipping God, particularly in the way we care for God's created realm. Because worshipping God and enjoying Him forever is the chief aim of humankind, discovering and living according to those biblical and theological principles that maximally display the glory of God are *the* most important elements of the debate. It is the purpose of this book, then, to demonstrate how Christian Scripture and theology ought to normatively motivate and guide Christ followers to become the sort of people who behave in a manner that honors the King of the universe by the way they treat and care for his universe.

II. Our Outline

In keeping with this purpose, then, the goal of chap. 1, "Finding True North," is threefold. First, we wish to introduce the reader to the primary metaphor shaping our discussion. Second, we seek to orient the reader to environmental ethics by offering a very brief (and entirely inadequate) history of the recent discussion. Third, it is our hope to show the need for a clear point of reference by which Christians can both guide and check their beliefs and practices related to all areas of life, but specifically to the area of environmental concern and creation care.

Chapter 2 begins our biblical and theological exploration of the doctrines of God and Christology and specifically the person of Jesus Christ and his role in the creation. The focus of discussion is Genesis 1 and 2. Chapter 3 continues this discussion by exploring the creation of human beings as image bearers and the purposes for which God created them. Scripturally, this chapter focuses more particularly on Gen 2:15 and Gen 1:27–28.

In chap. 4, it is our purpose to explore the role of Jesus Christ as the incarnate and resurrected Redeemer. We begin this discussion by developing Genesis 3 and the fall as it relates to the entire created order. We then discuss how the gospel of Jesus Christ is the central controlling element of a properly understood Christian perspective on creation care.

In chap. 5, we then consider the role of Jesus Christ as the future coming King and the One who will bring a full transformation to the created order. In this chapter we contrast rival views of the future, briefly discuss the biblical teaching on the second coming of Christ, explore the transformation of the earth promised in 2 Pet 3:3–10, and then conclude the chapter with a discussion of the resurrection of the body promised at the Day of the Lord.

Finally, in chap. 6, "Pursuing True North," we begin by reviewing each component of the argument up to that point, and then suggest an overarching ethical schemata and methodology that we believe ought to function as the frame of reference for all of life—and specifically for issues related to creation care. Having done so, we will move to a conclusion by arguing that a truly Christian perspective on creation care must always be a matter of pursuing God in Christ as the ultimate point of orientation for the universe, and then purposefully and rigorously determining to align ourselves, the community of faith, the human race, and all of creation to that end.

Finding True North

It is quite interesting and not a little ironic that the new ecotheologies often start not by discussing God, faith, tradition, or the holy, but with references to information provided by biologists, chemists, and ecologists.[1]

I. Introduction: True North

Imagine it is the middle of the night and you are on a boat far out at sea in uncharted waters. You are adrift and uncertain of where to go. Rising winds and strange currents are pushing you aimlessly as you see the flashes of a storm flickering on the horizon.

In the early days of nautical travel, sailors would face such situations without sophisticated radio equipment or GPS tracking systems. Indeed, because they lacked such navigational tools, it was typical for sailors to chart their course by staying within sight of land and using recognizable landmarks. This worked fine, of course, until they forsook the safety of the coastline and pushed beyond the horizon. No longer able to see the familiar landmarks, they needed to find a new point of reference. And thus, they looked to the heavens.

By gazing at the night sky, sailors eventually learned that although most of the stars appeared to move, one remained constant: Polaris, the North Star. Because it appeared fixed in the heavens, it became the sailors' most trusted advisor. With the aid of navigational tools like the sextant and compass, sailors could not only pinpoint their current position; they could also determine the proper course necessary to reach their destination.

---

1. Roger S. Gottlieb, *A Greener Faith: Religious Environmentalism and Our Planet's Future* (New York: Oxford University Press, 2006), 20.

Now imagine what would happen to a sailor if he or she either chose to navigate merely by an "inner sense" of feel, by the general consensus of the crew, or by choosing the wrong star as the point of reference. In each case it would be entirely possible for the captain to *believe* with all certainty that he was charting the right course. But the belief would most likely not match up with reality. Even if the captain were convinced, such a conviction would in no way guarantee reaching the desired destination. Most likely, if he acted on his convictions without first ordering them to *True North*, even his rightly intended convictions would probably lead to loss or shipwreck.

We believe this is a good metaphor for understanding the current nature of much of the modern debates raging in all areas of ethics. Whether the issues involve the taking of life in war, capital punishment, abortion, or questions of sexuality and marriage, we live in a time and in a culture that questions the validity of any fixed reference point. Because of that, we find ourselves in a context in which it is becoming more and more difficult to arrive at a proper evaluation of our moral position. It is even more difficult to arrive at a consensus on how to chart a course in a direction that truly leads to holistic flourishing. Certainly the field of environmental ethics and creation care is no exception.

The fact that we now live in a world morally adrift is hard to dispute. But this was not always the case. When God created the universe, he did so with great love and precision. He also was careful to provide a foundational locus and direction by which the primary caretakers he put into the created order could properly navigate a moral course that was fully pleasing to himself. Further, this God-given moral course would also ensure the flourishing of the entire created realm. In more contemporary language, we would say that Adam and Eve had a proper conceptual framework by which they correctly perceived, interpreted, and judged their reality. That is, their worldview was calibrated to *True North*.[2]

In right relationship to God, nonsinful humanity was given the task to navigate a course for themselves and all creation that would rightly honor God and represent his best interests for the entire created realm. Not only were they given instruction; most importantly they also enjoyed the relational context with God by which they could both rightly and properly order, serve, protect, and orient God's world as an act of obedient worship.

2. Mark Liederbach and Alvin Reid, *The Convergent Church: Missional Worship in an Emerging Culture* (Grand Rapids, MI: Kregel, 2009), 32.

Tragically, it was because of human sin and rebellion that the long history of muddled moral thinking and acting followed. Instead of tracking a course to flourishing and joy, the legacy of humanity is one of moral drift and uncertainty. The reason for this is that with sin and rebellion came a fundamental shift in worldview. Our moral compass was no longer calibrated to *True North*. Inferior ends and ideas replaced those which humans were created to know and follow (Romans 1).

As Al Wolters points out,

> A worldview, even when it is half unconscious and unarticulated, functions like a compass or a road map. It orients us in the world at large, gives us a sense of what is up and what is down, what is right and what is wrong in the confusion of events and phenomena that confronts us. Our worldview shapes, to a significant degree, the way we assess the events, issues, and structures of our civilization and our times.[3]

Indeed, one of the basic facts of reality is that as human beings

> we cannot do without the kind of orientation and guidance that a worldview gives. We need guidance because we are inescapably creatures with responsibilities who by nature are incapable of holding purely arbitrary opinion or making entirely unprincipled decisions. We need some creed to live by, some map by which to chart our course. The need for a guiding perspective is basic to human life, perhaps more basic than food or sex.[4]

This fact is what makes living in a fallen world so perilous. Each of us individually, and all of humanity corporately, attempt to navigate through life with a broken compass. Indeed, in this postmodern era, the normative idea is that we cannot know whether there even is a *True North*. Therefore, as we pilot our ships, the best we can do is choose a course with conviction and learn to get along with the other passengers. Yet ultimately we are told we can have no certainty of where we are headed.

We hope the danger of this postmodern thinking is self-evident. A compass should be calibrated not by the searcher's preferences but by a certain and fixed reference point external to the self. That is, one must find *True North* first, calibrate the compass to that point, and then chart a course toward life and flourishing. To attempt to orient one's life or the

---

3. Albert M. Wolters, *Creation Regained: Biblical Basis for a Reformational Worldview,* 2nd ed. (Grand Rapids, MI: Eerdmans, 2005), 5.

4. Ibid.

culture's moral path by simply choosing a direction that seems reasonable and then calling a robust pursuit of that end a viable option to *True North* is fundamentally silly.

James Davidson Hunter's argument in his *To Change the World* makes a similar point. He argues that while humans use power to shape the world in which they live, they do so while they are "instinctually challenged" (i.e., morally decrepit). This is not to say that humans use their power without direction. To the contrary, because Wolters is correct in asserting that everyone has a worldview whether they know it or not; people always function from some frame of reference. The problem that then emerges is that humans wield world-shaping power without a clear and coherent worldview, point of reference, or properly determined end goal. Yet because worldviews always head in some direction, human use of power (either individually or collectively) will shape the world in whatever direction their moral compass is pointing.

> What is power then? Power is not a substance or a property but a facility that is exercised in relation to others as well as, of course, to the natural world. This facility manifests itself through individuals, through social groups of every size, shape and kind, through social structures . . . and through our own subjectivity. It is within every institution, and not just the institutions of government or market. It is through power that worlds are created—the larger cultures of which we are a part and our own personal worlds shared with those closest to us.[5]

Clearly, then, the foundational ideas one holds at the conviction level—explicitly or implicitly—are vitally important.

For the Christian,

> what this means is that faithful Christian witness is fated to exist in the tension between the historical and the transcendent; between the social realities that press on human existence and the spiritual and ethical requirements of the gospel; between the morality of the society in which Christian believers live and the will of God. These oppositions are a fact of existence for the church and each Christian believer and they pull in conflicting directions—one toward the necessities of survival and the other toward the perfect will of God. There is no place of

---

5. James Davidson Hunter, *To Change the World* (New York: Oxford University Press, 2010), 179.

equilibrium between these oppositions and no satisfying resolutions. In this world, the church can never be in repose.[6]

For these reasons it is utterly important that each of us (and all of us corporately) pay careful attention to how we are calibrating our compasses. Scripture is clear. All things have been created by God, through God, and for God, and they are created for his glory (Rom 11:36). Therefore, although it be tempting to calibrate the compass toward such noble ends as "saving the planet" or "living a good life," ultimately the pursuit of anything other than Christ is foolish both temporally and eternally. Biblically and theologically speaking, these (and/or any other goals) are in essence idolatrous. They set an inferior end in the place of the ultimate end for which God created the world. It is imperative, then, that we calibrate our compasses to Jesus Christ and set our course toward a pursuit of the One who is the *True North* of the created order, the redeemed creation, and the future fully established eschatological kingdom.

II. Environmental Ethics and Creation Care

This, of course, brings us directly to the reason why our discussion of environmental ethics and the Christian's concern for creation care is so important. The fundamental ideas that form the foundations of the movement ultimately form a vision of the world and its purpose and that will, in turn, drive the moral conclusions and calls for action in a particular direction and toward some type of end. For this reason a brief history and description of key perspectives in the contemporary environmental movement can help our readers evaluate the underlying ideas at play in the larger cultural discussion as well as see the value of this overall project.

Three Predominant Perspectives Shaping the Secular Landscape

In the most general sense, environmental ethics has evolved from a counterculture movement to a major social issue in a relatively short period of time.[7] Andrew Light and Holmes Rolston III aptly describe this shift in the following manner:

---

6. Ibid., 183.

7. It is important to note here that Santmire and others have demonstrated that within the Christian tradition, there is a consistent stream of thought about the value of nature as far back as the patristic era. Therefore, this statement is not to be construed to mean that environmental concern

While one can trace roots in the field back much further, explicitly and implicitly in the work of philosophers and non-philosophers alike, the first articles in philosophy journals specifically on environmental topics, the first books, the first conferences and the first classes in colleges and universities all began in the early 1970s. This was no coincidence. The environmental movement was then transforming from its earlier phase consisting mainly in practical resource conservation initiatives, such as the creation of the national park system, to a much more active political and social force in its own right.[8]

This progression from minor conservation movement to major social issue has catapulted environmental ethics from the "applied ethics" category of philosophy to the level of interdisciplinary field of study.[9] A prime example of its growing popularity not only in the field of philosophy but also in mainstream culture is the immense success of two recent films, *An Inconvenient Truth* (2006) and *Wall-E* (2008). These films focus on core components of what has now become the bedrock of environmental ethics—the need to *do* something about "the problem" of the environment and the intrinsic value of nature, respectively.[10]

---

did not exist prior to the countercultural movement of the 1960s. See Paul Santmire, *The Travail of Nature: The Ambiguous Ecological Promise of Christian Theology* (Philadelphia, PA: Fortress, 1985).

8. Andrew Light and Holmes Rolston III, eds., *Environmental Ethics: An Anthology* (Malden, MA: Blackwell, 2003), 1. Louis P. Pojman, *Environmental Ethics: Readings in Theory and Application*, 2nd ed. (Belmont, CA: Wadsworth, 1998), vii, gives a more dated but contextual view of this shift with this description, stating, "I remember searching through journals for relevant articles, usually without much success. Not many environmental courses (I knew of none) were being offered in the late 1970s when I requested permission from my university to offer such a course. My colleagues questioned whether there was a need for such a 'soft,' non-traditional course and whether enough material existed to put a syllabus together. . . . Today, some 20 years later, environmental ethics is a burgeoning field. Courses in this subject are taught in most universities in the United States, and books and articles appear almost weekly." See also Dieter Hessel and Larry Rasmussen, eds., *Earth Habitat: Eco-Injustice and the Church's Response* (Minneapolis, MN: Fortress, 2001), 30.

9. Eugene Hargrove, *Foundations of Environmental Ethics* (Denton, TX: Environmental Ethics Books, 1989), 2. Hargrove shows how environmental ethics has bypassed the "applied ethics" level because it incorporates components of more established fields within philosophy. Interestingly, he concludes that "whereas the other parts of applied ethics will likely remain distinct subject areas, as sub-disciplines in philosophy, I expect that eventually environmental ethics will disappear as the various mainstream subject areas adjust and take account of the problems environmental ethics deals with. In other words, when the environment is properly taken into account in the basic fields within philosophy, there will be little need for environmental ethics as a distinct subject." Twenty-two years later, this is hardly the case on the contemporary scene.

10. Karl Burkhart, "Top 10 Environmental Films of All Time," n.p. [accessed 15 June 2011]. Online: http://www.mnn.com/green-tech/research-innovations/blogs/top-10-environmental-films-of-all-time. Burkhart, a writer for the website of the *Mother Nature Network,* develops this list of influential films to demonstrate the power that film has over politics and culture. As a demonstration of the growing interest in this field, six of the ten movies listed were released after 2000. See also Michael Cieply, "On Screens Soon, Abused

Along the way, several different metaethical approaches have developed that are characteristic of both mainstream and Christian environmental ethics. For the purposes of this book, we will briefly focus in this section on the three most popular secular approaches: biocentrism, anthropocentrism, and ecocentrism.

Biocentrism is predicated on the notion that all living organisms (human and nonhuman) have an inherent, noninstrumental value. More specifically, DesJardins defines biocentricism as "any theory that views all life as possessing intrinsic value."[11] An early version of the biocentric approach to environmental ethics can be found in the work of Albert Schweitzer.[12] However, Schweitzer's theory was not considered by most to be scholarly enough and was consequently never popularized. Some 40 years later, Paul Taylor took Schweitzer's work and constructed a full theory of biocentrism which is based on the following four premises:

(a) The belief that humans are members of the Earth's Community of Life in the same sense and on the same terms in which other living things are members of that Community.

(b) The belief that the human species, along with all other species, are integral elements in a system of interdependence such that the survival of each living thing, as well as its chances of faring well or poorly, is determined not only by the physical conditions of its environment but also by its relations to other living things.

(c) The belief that all organisms are teleological centers of life in the sense that each is a unique individual pursuing its own good in its own way.

(d) The belief that humans are not inherently superior to other living things.[13]

Earth Gets Its Revenge," n.p. [accessed 15 June 2011]. Online: http://www.nytimes.com/ 2007/03/12/movies/12vill.html; Robin L. Murray and Joseph K. Heumann, *Ecology and Popular Film: Cinema on the Edge* (Albany, NY: SUNY Press, 2009).

11. Joseph DesJardins, *Environmental Ethics* (Florence, KY: Wadsworth, 2006), 131. See also Thomas Derr, *Environmental Ethics and Christian Humanism*, vol. 2 of Abingdon Press Studies in Christian Ethics and Economic Life, ed. Max Stackhouse (Nashville, TN: Abingdon, 1996). Derr suggests that animal rights activists, eco-feminists, and those adhering to James Lovelock's "Gaia Hypothesis" practice forms of biocentricism (36–62).

12. Albert Schweitzer, *Civilization and Ethics* (London: A. & C. Black, 1946). This is easily his most comprehensive metaethical presentation. Schweitzer was convinced that nature contains goodness and declared it to have intrinsic value relative to that goodness. He encapsulated his theory in the phrase "reverence for life." See also Stephen Bouma-Prediger, *For the Beauty of the Earth: A Christian Vision for Creation Care*, 2nd ed. (Grand Rapids, MI: Baker, 2010), 123.

13. Paul Taylor, *Respect for Nature: A Theory of Environmental Ethics* (Princeton, NJ: Princeton University Press, 1986), 99–100.

From a biocentric perspective, then, humans are unique among created beings but are not inherently of any more value. In short, there is nothing unique about human beings being unique. Ironically, though, there is a tendency among biocentrists to elevate noneudaimonistic flourishing (flourishing of nonhumans) above eudaimonistic flourishing (flourishing of humans).

Ecocentrism is similar to biocentric ethics in the sense that it focuses on the interconnectedness of nature and is nonanthropocentric. However, it is ultimately much more inclusive than biocentrism. This essentially means that ecocentric environmental ethics takes into consideration not only life (biocentrism) but also that which is considered lifeless, such as ecosystems or the biosphere as a whole. This position is most often identified with the land ethic espoused by Aldo Leopold and is sometimes referred to as ethical holism.[14] DesJardins's work is helpful in understanding this position, especially as it is distinct from the biocentric position. DesJardins argues that there are three different types of ecocentrism (ecocentric holism). First, there is a metaphysical holism, which claims that wholes are real, perhaps more real than their constituent parts. This is generally the position of Leopold, Callicott, and Rolston. Second, there is a methodological or epistemological holism, which focuses on how best to understand various phenomena concerning the ecosystem. The third category is labeled ethical holism and suggests that moral considerability should be extended to wholes.[15]

The final position differs significantly from the first two positions and is labeled *anthropocentrism*. The focus of anthropocentric environmental ethics is on human beings and their value over and above the value of all other nature whether living or not. From the anthropocentric viewpoint, nature has merely instrumental value and exists to serve the greater good and purposes of human beings. DesJardins defines this position as one in which humans "may be said to have responsibilities *regarding* the natural world" but do not have "direct responsibilities *to* the natural world."[16] This particular position is most often defended in light of responsibilities to future generations.[17]

This position has been the most unpopular position among secular environmentalists who believe that the current plight of the biosphere

14. Aldo Leopold, *A Sand County Almanac and Sketches Here and There* (Oxford, UK: Oxford University Press, 1949).

15. DesJardins, *Environmental Ethics*, 170–71.

16. Ibid., 12.

17. See, for example, Mary Anne Warren, "Future Generations," in *And Justice for All*, ed. Tom Regan and Donald VanDeVeer (Totowa, NJ: Rowman and Littlefield, 1982).

is a result of anthropocentric thinking.[18] However, this does not mean that there have not been attempts to defend this position so as to offer it as a legitimate alternative to the dominant biocentric and ecocentric worldviews. Eugene Hargrove, for instance, is sympathetic to the noninstrumental nonanthropocentric position but argues that not all anthropocentric theories have to be instrumental in nature. He writes,

> There are, first of all, innumerable instrumental relationships in natural systems that are completely independent of any possible instrumental value to human beings, and these (or similar) nonanthropocentric instrumental values would exist whether humans had ever evolved and will continue to exist even after humans become extinct, so long as life itself persists.[19]

It is Hargrove's contention that an anthropocentric intrinsic value argument is possible and can be supported by looking to the history of ideas that formulated environmental ethics.[20]

Three Predominant Perspectives Shaping the Evangelical Landscape

With a brief survey of the secular scene completed, we can turn our attention to the Christian environmental ethics arena. In light of the growing popularity and the reality that environmentalism has become a dominant social issue,[21] Christians are increasingly realizing that they must engage this issue intelligently or run the risk of becoming irrelevant.[22]

Beginning with Francis Schaeffer in his *Pollution and the Death of Man* (1970), a growing number of evangelical Christians have attempted to motivate the greater Christian community towards engagement in the larger environmental conversation. While it is true that Schaeffer and many of the early writers were prompted in part to answer the criticisms

---

18. James Sterba has made an attempt to reconcile anthropocentric and nonanthropocentric environmental ethics in what could be interpreted as a defense of anthropocentric environmental ethics. See "Reconciling Anthropocentric and Nonanthropocentric Environmental Ethics," in *Earth Ethics: Environmental Ethics, Animal Rights, and Practical Applications*, ed. James Sterba (Englewood Cliffs, NJ: Prentice Hall, 1995), 199–213.

19. Hargrove, *Foundations of Environmental Ethics*, 10.

20. Ibid.

21. Holmes Rolston III, "Ethics on the Home Planet," in *An Invitation to Environmental Philosophy*, ed. Anthony Weston (New York: Oxford University Press, 1999), 138.

22. Francis Schaeffer, *Pollution and the Death of Man: The Christian View of Ecology* (Wheaton, IL: Tyndale House, 1970), 82.

that laid blame for the world's ecological problems at the feet of Christianity, more recently the creation care debate has evolved into a multifaceted discussion of stewardship, discipleship, and ethical responsibilities.[23] It is beyond the scope of this work to discuss in detail the work of every author who has contributed to this academic field. However, in his recent doctoral project, Donnie McDaniel nicely summarizes the three predominant perspectives that shape the evangelical landscape on the environment and creation care. McDaniel argues that though Christianity has produced its share of biocentric, ecocentric, and theocentric proposals, evangelicals have tended to remain in one of three camps he describes as *dominionists, dependents,* or *stewards.*[24] He goes on to both define each of these categories and to identify evangelicals who adopt these respective positions.

Dominionists, he argues, choose to build their theological ethic of creation care by focusing primarily on the commands given to Adam in Gen 1:26–28. By doing so they then formulate a response to the environmental crisis that focuses on humanity's call to have dominion over the rest of the created order.[25] E. Calvin Beisner and Thomas Sieger Derr are good examples of evangelicals whose positions reflect this perspective.

Other evangelical thinkers, however, formulate an approach that focuses primarily on the commands given to Adam in Gen 2:15. By taking this approach, the emphasis of their thinking then centers on the interrelatedness of life and humanity's dependence on the created order. This position then emphasizes mankind's obligation to serve the created order upon which it depends for survival. Thus, McDaniel appropriately labels it the *Dependence* model.[26] Two of the leading evangelicals thinking and writing from this perspective are Ted Hiebert and Wesley-Granberg Michaelson.

23. Lynn White Jr., "The Historical Roots of Our Ecological Crisis," in *Science* 155, no. 3767 (March 10, 1967). Accessible on the Internet at http://www.zbi.ee/~kalevi/lwhite.htm. We offer a reply to White later in chap. 3 of this book. Among the many authors to consider, we will highlight a few: Eric Rust, *Nature—Garden or Desert* (Waco, TX: Word Books, 1971); Calvin B. DeWitt, ed., *The Environment and the Christian: What Does the New Testament Say About the Environment?* (Grand Rapids, MI: Baker, 1991); Loren Wilkinson, *Earthkeeping in the Nineties* (Grand Rapids, MI: Eerdmans, 1991); Michael Northcott, *The Environment and Christian Ethics* (Grand Rapids, MI: Baker Academic, 2004); Bouma-Prediger, *For the Beauty of the Earth*; Noah J. Toly and Daniel I. Block, eds., *Keeping God's Earth: The Global Environment in Biblical Perspective* (Downers Grove, IL: IVP Academic, 2010); Allen Verhey, *The Great Reversal: Ethics and the New Testament* (Grand Rapids, MI: Eerdmans, 2010).
24. Donald R. McDaniel Jr., "Becoming Good Shepherds: A New Model of Creation Care for Evangelical Christians" (Ph.D. diss., Southeastern Baptist Theological Seminary, 2011), 2.
25. Ibid.
26. Ibid.

Most evangelicals, however, cannot be placed comfortably in either of these camps. Instead, McDaniel argues,

> the majority of evangelicals have supported another model that places equal emphasis on both sets of commands given to humans in the opening chapters of Genesis. This approach, called the *Stewardship* model, focuses on humanity as "stewards" or "just kings" that are charged to watch over all the gifts in creation while still remembering that the earth remains the permanent property of the Lord God, and that this God will hold his image bearing creature responsible for their stewardship over creation.[27]

Stephen Bouma-Prediger, Cal DeWitt, Richard Young, and Don Brandt are examples of evangelical scholars who fall into this category.

With these three predominant approaches to creation care among evangelicals in mind, we are persuaded that a form of the *stewardship* model ought to serve as the basis from which to develop an ethic of creation care. We believe, however, that such a model must also place the idea of stewardship directly in a theological ethic that emphasizes the centrality of worship to all we say, think, do, and act (see 1 Cor 10:31). The importance of adopting this type of model, we trust, will become evident in the following pages of this chapter and throughout the remainder of the book. In keeping with this, then, we believe it appropriate to turn our attention to a bit of critical analysis related to the moral motivations that are often in play and which result from the various philosophical and/or theological discussions that drive action or interest related to environmentalism and creation care.

III. Idolatry and the Loss of Direction in the Larger Debate

As the previous section attempted to demonstrate, there is a growing amount of attention being given to the field of environmental ethics. And while there are many nuances related to the differing views, underneath it seems that the conversation is often dominated by two "false views" that Father Robert A. Sirico rightly assesses as an inappropriate or "muddled" understanding of the relationship between God, Man, and nature. He writes, "The one sees the natural world as the source of all value, man as

---

27. Ibid.

intruder, and God, if he exists at all, as so immanent in the natural order that he ceases to be distinguishable from it. The other places man as the source of all values, the natural order as merely instrumental to his aims, and God as often irrelevant."[28]

Father Sirico's assessment is an insightful, particular description of a more general theological point Reformation theologian John Calvin advanced centuries ago: the human heart and mind function as a perpetual factory of idolatry.[29] On the one hand, in the context of environmental ethics and creation care discussions, human beings will have a tendency to make an idol out of things created. In the first chapter of the book of Romans, Paul described it this way:

> For since the creation of the world His invisible attributes, His eternal power and divine nature, have been clearly seen, being understood through what has been made, so that they are without excuse. For even though they knew God, they did not honor Him as God or give thanks, but they became futile in their speculations, and their foolish heart was darkened. Professing to be wise, they became fools, and exchanged the glory of the incorruptible God for an image in the form of corruptible man and of birds and four-footed animals and crawling creatures. (Rom 1:20–23)

Many of the *biocentric* and *ecocentric* proposals offer moral systems that describe the natural order in terms that personify nature or even deify it. Indeed, some suggest that the natural order is a self-aware entity that functionally takes on a transcendent importance in a manner strongly resembling ancient pagan ideas of Divine Nature or the pantheism of Eastern religions and mystical thought.

On the other hand, when humankind outright rejects the existence of God (or describes him as unknowable) and places itself at the center and source of all moral values, then we make idols of ourselves (individually or corporately) and our own reasoning capacities. This is perhaps the dominant legacy of those elements of Enlightenment thinking that rejected the possibility of God as the Creator of all things and the source of certain moral knowledge. Objective moral standards and ethical systems affirming a natural law and a divine revelation were slowly but surely replaced by a spirit of pragmatism determined by a utilitarian

---

28. Robert A. Sirico, "Foreword," in *Environmental Stewardship in the Judeo-Christian Tradition*, produced by The Acton Institute (Grand Rapids, MI: Acton Institute for the Study of Religion and Liberty, 2007), vii.

29. John Calvin, *The Institutes of the Christian Religion*, I.XI.8–9.

calculus. Moral certainties like the Ten Commandments were replaced by a human reasoning that suggests morality should be determined by ideas like "the greatest good for the greatest number of people" or "the ends justify the means." And now, as we slip into a philosophical era known as postmodernity, this form of reasoning takes on a more communal aspect in which a global community must come together to determine by consensus what is the "greatest good" and then provide the laws that best enforce the path to this supposed "greatest good."[30] Clearly this is the form of idolatry present in the anthropocentric views of environmentalism.

It is for this reason we would strongly disagree with Lynn White Jr.'s accusations against Christianity, which we will discuss more fully in chap. 3. While Christians certainly are not blameless, it is not the Christian worldview that is to blame but the legacy of the Enlightenment that ushered in power and abuse. For the Enlightenment ideas removed God and placed human reason as central to the moral endeavor, which in turn led to the conclusion that overconsumption of the earth's abundant natural resources would lead to the "greatest good." As we learned from Wolters and Hunter earlier is this chapter, those who held positions of power through wealth or influence used that power in accordance with their worldview. From an inferior worldview the use of power then often took the form of overconsumption and the accumulation of wealth by irresponsible and shortsighted exploitation of the earth's resources. Now, as the abundance of natural resources diminishes, there is the growing possibility of using power and influence in a manner that shifts from an anthropocentric form of idolatry to a perspective that deifies nature and seeks to protect it at all costs. To quote a classic rock song by The Who: "Meet the new boss, same as the old boss." In both extremes, idolatrous thinking rules the day. And in either form this idolatry of the heart is essentially a rejection of supremacy of the Triune Creator God. Thus, such views fall under proper assessment by the words of the ancient king of Israel, David, who said in Ps 14:1, "The fool has said in his heart, 'There is no God.'" May it be that as natural resources become scarcer and the environmental movement becomes more politically potent, we will become wise and virtuous people who revere the instruction of the Lord so that "we don't get fooled again."[31]

---

30. For a fuller version of this philosophical discussion and the effects of Enlightenment thinking on morality and culture, see Liederbach and Reid, *The Convergent Church*, 31–116.

31. Lyrics by Pete Townsend, "Won't Get Fooled Again," *Who's Next*, The Who (1971, AISN: B000002O7).

IV. Christian Debates and Temptations

While the two streams of idolatry identified above are very real tendencies among those who do not claim allegiance to the Christian faith, it is important to realize that even within the realm of Christianity, perspectives on the environment can vary widely. As a general stereotype, there are two rival *street-level* motivations that tend to shape how Christians respond to calls for environmental action. We will try to explain these polarized views by using the metaphor of two very different birds and then seek to demonstrate why both of these perspectives are insufficient for a follower of Christ to use as the primary motivating factors for his or her level of engagement on this issue.[32]

On the one hand, there are those who are convinced that we are in the midst of (or at least on the verge of) a massive worldwide environmental crisis. Thus, like "Chicken Little," in the classic children's fable, their conviction is that, environmentally speaking, the "sky is falling."[33] Because they believe there is a very real ecological cataclysm threatening on the horizon, they argue that environmental concern and creation care initiatives must become the number one social issue into which Christians ought to pour their energies.

On the other hand, there is a large contingency of skeptics who tend to outright deny (or some would say "live in denial of") the urgency of the entire matter. Like the proverbial ostrich that sticks its head in the sand when danger approaches, this group is said to deny the possibility (and "proof") that an environmental crisis is at hand. They either are so skeptical of the claim that environmental problems are at critical levels or are so convinced a solution will be found, that they refuse to make any changes to beliefs or practices. Typically, they are also not interested enough (for a variety of reasons) to give the time and energy necessary to discover what truth, if any, exists in "Chicken Little's" claims.

---

32. We want to thank Dr. Bruce A. Little for providing us with this comparative metaphor at the "Creation Care: A Theology of Stewardship" conference held at the L. Russ Bush Center for Faith and Culture on October 30–31, 2009. See http://www.sebts.edu/faithandculture/events/creation_care_conf.aspx

33. *The Sky Is Falling*, better known as *Chicken Licken, Henny Penny* or *Chicken Little,* is an old fable about a chicken (or a hare in early versions) who believes the sky is falling. The phrase, "The sky is falling," has passed into the English language as a common idiom indicating "a hysterical or mistaken belief that disaster is imminent." See http://en.wikipedia.org/wiki/The_Sky_Is_Falling_(fable).

An example of this perspective can be found in Tony Campolo, *How to Rescue the Earth Without Worshipping Nature: A Christian's Call to Save Creation* (Waco, TX: Word, 1992). He even titles a chapter in his early work on the environment "Chicken Little Was Right."

It should come as no surprise that these two birds tend not to get along.

Chicken Littles and the Problems with Crisis Motivation

One of the main reasons these differing perspectives (and the resulting animosities) exist has to do with a similar level of conviction for moral issues but a disagreement on which issues deserve primary attention. The Chicken Littles are convinced that *human-caused environmental degra-dations* pose an immediate threat. Therefore, for them it is a matter of survival that we mobilize immediate action to protect and restore God's creation. And because the perceived urgency of this task is so intense, these folks often become immensely frustrated with those "Ostriches" who do not share their level of conviction.

For this reason, there is a temptation for Chicken Littles to find allies and cobelligerents in the battle to save the planet with those who are either non-Christian or with "Christians" who may hold to a variety of convictions about the nature of God as well as suspect understandings on the nature of Scripture and the person and work of Christ. The danger, of course, is such allegiances (even if one holds closely to core orthodox doctrines in their view of salvation) tend to invite criticisms related to "watering down the gospel." Guilt by association is a real danger here. Often these theologically orthodox, good-hearted Chicken Littles are simply lumped into a category of liberal-minded or "drifting" Christians who are giving up their orthodoxy and the proper focus on evangelism for the sake of spotted owls.[34]

Of even greater importance (assuming this group of believers stays true to orthodox teaching—as many do) is the problem of crisis-moti-vated ethics. Clearly, if one has paid any attention to the modern debates among Christians and non-Christians alike, much of the disagreement that takes place stems from the uncertainty and varying perspectives on how to interpret the scientific data available related to the actual state of the planet and debated levels of environmental degradation.

Right or wrong, the lack of consensus within the religious, scientific, economic, and political realms understandably leaves many who are less

---

34. For an interesting example of this, see Tony Campolo's *How to Rescue the Earth Without Worshipping Nature*. We personally have many points of disagreement with Dr. Campolo in other areas of ethics, but we find his discussion on this point fascinating. He relates in the opening chapters of this book how by his merely speaking to this issue he had to defend his orthodoxy among more conservative friends.

trained in the nuances of these debates wondering whether the incessant cry that the "sky is falling" is simply overhyped. This is why, in part, we would suggest that a crisis mentality and argument is ultimately not the best way to address the issue of creation care nor serve as the *primary motivation* for believers to act. While concern for the environment can certainly play a role in *catalyzing* response, acting from a crisis modality is problematic. Consider the following seven reasons we believe this is so.

First, while few deny that some level of environmental degradation is taking place, much disagreement exists as to the level of severity. Not only are the conclusions of the scientific models "proving" the crisis under debate; disagreements also abound as to what might be the best economic model and/or political action to solve the problem. It is hard to motivate people to solve a problem if they do not agree it exists or if they believe the offered solutions are flawed.

Second, underlying the use of crisis as a primary motivation is the reality that fear becomes the primary motivating emotion. While we have no doubt that fear is indeed a strong motivator, we do have reservations about allowing fear to drive Christian thinking. God's perfect love is meant to cast out fear (1 John 4:18). Thus, Christians in particular, must be very careful not to give in to the temptation of motivating to action via crisis thinking, since this undermines a trust in God in the face of all circumstances.

Third, crisis motivation is ultimately anemic. If the crisis is solved or is perceived as unwinnable, then the moral imperative for life and character change ceases to exist.

Fourth, crisis-driven motivation ultimately arises from (and fosters) an anthropocentric model of ethics and creation care. That is, when crisis is the focus, more often than not, the fundamental reason it is understood as a crisis is the potential effect it will have on humans. Even for those who claim to have a theocentric or even biocentric disposition underlying their ethic, typically the argument becomes focused on how the crisis will be bad for humans if we do not change.[35] While it may very well be the case that any environmental crisis will affect humanity greatly, we simply ask if for the Christian this should be our primary concern? Should possible negative consequences be the primary motivational drive

---

35. For a fuller treatment of this issue within the emerging environmental ethics movement, please see Seth A. Bible, "Pursuing Ecological Virtue: A Critical Analysis of the Environmental Virtue Ethics Models of Ronald Sandler, Louke Van Wensveen, and Philip Cafaro" (Ph.D. diss., Southeastern Baptist Theological Seminary, 2011).

to behave in a certain manner? We will give more attention to this in a moment.

Fifth, if *the crisis* becomes the primary ethical motivator, then the drive to "solve the crisis" will tend to push toward the enactment of "whatever means is necessary" utilitarianism. In other words, crisis motivation will always *tend toward* the adoption of an "ends justify the means" moral utilitarian calculus that can very easily be used to sidestep and compromise biblical standards of obedience, ethics, and worship. For example, if overpopulation is a key element in an environmental crisis, then how long will it be before the issue of abortion is considered as a means to and justifiable manner for solving the problem? As we are sure many of our readers have already deduced, in many parts of the world this is already the case.

Sixth, and following from the previous three reasons, once a "solve the crisis" ethical model is adopted, then focus on character change will tend to take a back seat to simple behavior modification in order to get through the crisis stage. From that point, as is the case with any act- and rule-based ethic, it is not a far step to the development of eco-legalism and enviro-judgmentalism. But should we not be concerned to deal primarily with the heart and internal motivations, idolatries, greed, virtues, and vices that drive our actions and shape our character?

Finally, as a bookend to the first point, our seventh reason is that a focus on crisis not only legitimates fear but in so doing actually distracts from the highest of Christian motivations: love-based worship of the Creator. Disciples of Jesus Christ ought to be motivated by an imitation of Christ and the worship given to him throughout the created realm. This is the kind of motivation that is and should be the *True North* for all ethical living.

In sum, then, we do not suggest that Christians should be unconcerned about consequences; rather, we are trying to emphasize that engaging the issue of creation care (or any moral issue) based on "crisis modality" will ultimately prove to be an inferior form of motivation to the rich biblical ethic that seeks to motivate action and behavior based on principles of conduct that shape a character in both individuals and the church that model conformity to the image of Christ. Crisis motivations rely on fear, whereas properly formed Christian ethics rely on a pursuit of fullness of joy in Christlike character founded in, and shaped by, worshipful obedience to God.

Ostriches and the Danger of Disembodied Doctrine

Having considered some of the concerns regarding the thinking of Chicken Littles, it is now appropriate to analyze the motivational elements of Ostriches. Those who deny the existence of such a crisis (or who are simply not yet convinced it is as bad as some claim) do not want to be distracted from what they perceive to be the more pressing mission for the church—primarily evangelism. As Christopher Wright describes it, "Christians sometimes feel anxious that 'the world is setting the agenda,' that is, that we simply respond to the flavor of the month in the changing fads of secular concerns. And it is certainly true that environmental concern is very high on the list of anxieties of the world today. Surveys of young people in the West often find that the very survival of planet Earth comes out at the top of the list of things they worry about."[36]

Christians may think like Ostriches for a number of reasons. First, some argue that the mission of the church is to focus on evangelism and not ethics. For this reason they do not stand opposed to those who would put effort into creation care, but at the same time they do not want this or any other ethical issue distracting the church from its primary mission of evangelism. For others there is an understanding that moral and social ethics issues are an important part of discipleship and moral witness, but it is their conviction that the more clear and present dangers are associated with moral issues of life and death (abortion, cloning, stem-cell research, euthanasia) and the foundational moral fabric of society (marriage, homosexuality, and other issues related to the separation of church and state). Because, they argue, these issues are already crisis issues and they are clear forms of *moral, societal, and ultimately, spiritual degradations,* we cannot afford to shift our attention, focus, and efforts away from first-order priorities of saving souls, saving lives, and saving society.

The temptation that faces this group is the tendency to unfairly stereotype anyone who has great concern and is motivated to care for the environment as being out of step with orthodoxy. They are tempted to label anyone who does not prioritize their convictions in the same manner as a "tree-hugger," on the verge of embracing pantheism, or someone who is backsliding into a "social gospel" understanding of Christianity.[37] Further, because many theologically and morally liberal Christians place

---

36. Christopher J. H. Wright, *The Mission of God* (Downers Grove, IL: IVP Academic, 2006), 417.

37. For further discussion on the history and struggles within evangelicalism related to the social gospel, please see chap. 9, "Who's Afraid of the Social Gospel?" in Liederbach and Reid, *The Convergent Church*.

great concern on environmentalism, those who are more conservative Christians face the temptation to oversimplify the issue, generalize, and lump together any and all who call for a prioritization of environmental concern into the category of "liberal." As mentioned earlier, there is a temptation to judge those with environmental concern as guilty by association.

The danger for those in this camp, then, has several elements. First, and of most importance, if Scripture and historical orthodox teaching indicate that followers of Jesus Christ *ought* to have a great concern for the care and stewardship of the created order, then we would be in disobedience to neglect this part of our discipleship.

Second, and related, if God is concerned with the way we treat and steward his possessions, then creation care and environmental concern, by definition, cannot be counter to a gospel witness for Jesus Christ. We will state clearly here and argue throughout this book that the proclamation of the gospel must remain both verbal and focused on the penal substitutionary nature of Christ's death and resurrection as the only means of personal salvation. However, as Scripture and church history have affirmed for two millennia, Christian action and moral behavior also serve as a witness to the lordship of Christ in all things. Thus, any moral issue—including creation care—should not be looked at in an either/or manner in regard to the gospel of Jesus Christ. There is a danger in giving ourselves over to the temptation to separate proclamation and ethics as distinct aspects of the Christian life. In this regard the Christian must think "both/and" rather than "either/or." Like the sanctity of human life or the covenant of marriage, if God cares deeply about how we treat and steward creation, not only must we care about it, but we must also understand it is a part of our gospel-centered moral witness to a watching world.

Third, an obvious danger for those who tend to deny the importance of being concerned about the environment is that the crisis may turn out to be real.[38] And if so, that is all the more reason not to be dismissive now. Certainly debates about public policy and economic solutions will (and should) continue. However, in regard to recognizing the importance of paying attention and entering the discussion in a concerned and

---

38. Please notice that the order in which we identify these three dangers is intentional. From what we believe to be a biblical and doctrinal perspective, while there is no question that pragmatics and consequences are an important aspect of the conversation, we do not believe they should be the driving elements of Christian ethics. We hope to make the reasons for this conviction clear throughout the content of this book.

informed manner, Christians ought to see this as a time to shine forth in word and deed.

In keeping with our earlier discussion, the motivation for involvement here would not be fear but, rather, a love for God and a love for his created order. Like it or not, this issue has garnered international attention. Evangelicals who are concerned to have a relevant and winsome gospel witness cannot afford to be decades behind the discussion. Crisis or not, the fact of the matter is that all Christians who love and care for the things that God loves and cares for—whether it be the life of a baby or the beauty of creation—honor God and potentially accelerate gospel influence by engaging any and all social issues with a gospel-centered heart and mind.

This brings us to the fourth point of danger for the "Ostrich" types. If they are not careful, they run the risk of disembodying the gospel. But for two millennia it has been the pattern of the Christian witness to couple verbal proclamation of the gospel message that Jesus is the Way, the Truth, and the Life, with ethical concern and action that address the pressing issues of humanity in that day and context. Thus, it is simply wise that Jesus' disciples step in and make a difference *for the sake of the gospel and the worship of Jesus Christ*. This is especially the case when an entire world is concerned about the issue at hand.

On a very pragmatic level, it should come as no surprise to any of us that differing perspectives on this issue exist. In fact, it is quite understandable—even if not ultimately acceptable. The first reason for this is that the church of Jesus Christ always feels a tension between the call to verbal proclamational evangelism and the moral imperative to do good works. The debate between faith and works (ultimately a false dichotomy) has raged since Paul (Eph 2:8–9) and James (Jas 2:18) wrote their epistles. Part of the struggle toward maturity for believers in any age and context is to learn how to integrate these elements of evangelism and discipleship into a unified whole.

Thus, for the maturing and ministering worshipper of God, every opportunity to speak or preach the message of the gospel is understood also as an opportunity to establish a God-honoring ethic in the life of an image bearer. Likewise, every opportunity to live ethically and honorably before the Lord is an opportunity to bring to light and preach the gospel of Jesus Christ.[39] This is "incarnational theology." These two elements

---

39. At this point we are at pains to emphasize that we reject any notion or claim that ethical action divorced from specific verbal proclamation of the person and saving work of Jesus Christ is by itself sufficient means of gospel proclamation. Verbal proclamation of the gospel message is

of following Christ *should never be seen as one-to-one substitutes for each other*. Rather, as believers grow in their faith and understanding of what it means to submit our lives to the supremacy of Christ in all things, we need to understand that ethics and evangelism *are two sides of the same coin*.[40]

V. Finding True North

Regardless of whether a person finds himself or herself identifying more with Chicken Littles, Ostriches, or any other group, one thing is clear: the uncertainty and intensity of this debate has pushed us all into uncharted waters. Not only is the issue of a global environmental crisis something humanity has never faced before, but the existence of a multitude of perspectives on how to interpret the data and what to do about it makes it even harder to determine how to move forward in the most God honoring way.

Thankfully, this type of predicament is nothing new for the church. Indeed, throughout church history, whenever any new doctrinal debate or social issue has taken center stage, the church, through its faithful allegiance to the Scriptures as the revealed Word of God and the guidance of the Holy Spirit, has always been able to chart a way forward in a manner pleasing to God. Frequently in doing so there was a lag time between the onset of the issue and the articulation of how the gospel ought to drive a Christian response.[41]

Thus, it is our conviction that focusing on the person of Christ and understanding his purposes in creating, redeeming, and eventually coming again to rule and reign over the earth is essential for any Christian who is serious about opening the doors to a gospel witness that is relevant to a watching world. Throughout the history of the church, no matter what the issue, it was by maintaining a clear focus on Christ as the ultimate point of reference that the proper way home was found.

Thus, returning to our dominant metaphor, finding ourselves in uncharted waters on the issue of environmental ethics and creation care,

---

an imperative for all believers. What we are arguing here, however, is that ethical behavior often prepares the way and opens the door for those evangelistic discussions. Further, we would argue that because God created the world, caring for it is good in its own right.

40. For further reading on this, see chaps. 5 and 6 of Liederbach and Reid, *The Convergent Church*.

41. This is why, for example, issues such as the doctrine of the Trinity or the divinity of Christ took years to develop via church councils and creeds. It was the context and debate of the time that drew out the need to emphasize points of faith and doctrine that fully present in the Scriptures but not yet emphasized in the community of faith—because the need had not yet materialized.

it is not only imperative that we find *True North*, but that we fix our eyes on it (him) and see our entire journey in light of the pursuit of it (him). Truly it would be foolish to attempt the journey any other way.

It is time for us to begin.

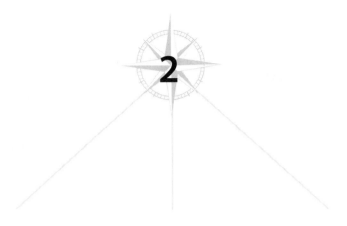

Christ the Creator of All Things

Nothing will so enlarge the intellect, nothing so magnify the whole soul of man, as a devout, earnest, continued, investigation of the great subject of the Deity. The most excellent study for expanding the soul is the science of Christ and Him crucified and the knowledge of the Godhead in the glorious Trinity.

Charles Spurgeon[1]

I. Introduction

As we highlighted earlier, there is a strong tendency within the environmental movement to motivate action via a crisis mentality. We highlighted several reasons why we believe that such a form of motivation—even if the crisis is as bad as some claim—is inadequate for the believer. We also hinted at our conviction that it is an inferior form of motivation relative to one based on a gospel-centered biblical theology of creation care. It is our intention in this chapter to set the foundation for understanding how and why knowing God himself is the crucial element in the entire discussion of creation care and environmental ethics. In order to do this, this chapter will engage the discussion by looking through a scriptural lens at the doctrine of God and the doctrine of creation.

To begin, we affirm A. W. Tozer's point that there is scarcely a problem with our ethics that is not ultimately traceable to our conception of God.[2] The reason Tozer is correct in this assertion is because Scripture

---

1. Charles Spurgeon, "Sermon on Malachi 3:6," quoted in Arthur W. Pink, *The Attributes of God* (Grand Rapids, MI: Baker, 1975), 88.
2. A. W. Tozer, *The Knowledge of the Holy* (San Francisco: Harper Collins, 1961), 2.

affirms that "in the beginning God created the heavens and the earth" (Gen 1:1). Further, from Scripture we learn that it is in God that "we live and move and have our being" (Acts 17:28). Because it is also true that "all things have been created by Him and for Him" (Col 1:16), then Dietrich Bonhoeffer was correct when he asserted that the fundamental question of Christian ethics is always one that addresses *who* prior to *how*.[3] In other words, a proper understanding of how one ought to live is dependent upon understanding who designed us, as well as the purpose for which God created the universe. Therefore, for the Christian, focusing on and understanding the nature and character of God is more foundational to shaping who we are and motivating what we do than any crisis that we may be facing. Indeed, the manner in which we face any situation in ethics—crisis or not—will be determined by our deeply held conviction about what we truly believe God to be like and what we hold to be true regarding the purposes for which he created all things.

II. Christ as the Ground and Source of Creation

Near the end of his life, Charles Darwin, the father of modern evolutionary theory, indicated that as he grew older, the joy he once found in nature began to turn dull. This is a fascinating reality. Here is the man who perhaps more than any other in modern thinking caused what Alister McGrath describes as the "disenchantment of nature" reaping in his personal affectations the fruits of his own worldview. This should come as no surprise when the fundamental tenets of his worldview include the idea that "the basic ethical consequences of scientific naturalism is that we don't matter to the universe."[4] Because Darwin's worldview proposed that nature is based only on impersonal matter plus time plus chance, it was virtually inevitable that he would experience a "death of joy."[5]

---

3. Dietrich Bonhoeffer, *Christology*, trans. John Bowden (London: Collins; New York: Harper & Row, 1966).

4. Bill Cooke, "Religion's Anthropocentric Conceit: Atheism's Cosmic Modesty Is More Moral," *Free Inquiry* 24, no.1 (December 2003/January 2004). Cited from http://secularhumanism.org/library/fi/cooke_24_1.htm.

5. Francis Schaeffer, *Pollution and the Death of Man* (Wheaton, IL: Crossway, 1970), 9–11. Indeed, we strongly agree with Schaeffer, McGrath, and a host of others who assert that contrary to Lynn White's now legendary accusation that Christianity is the source of the modern ecological crisis, it was modernity and its embracing of enlightenment thinking that replaced the Christian Trinity with the trinity of reason, naturalism (evolution), and progress that is to blame. In McGrath's words, "Far from bringing joy, the Enlightenment has led to the slow death of nature—and perhaps us with it. For among the 'taboos' and 'superstitions' swept away by the Enlightenment were the ideas that there were limits to human action within the world, and that nature, as God's creation, should be respected and honored. We are now paying the price for that loss." See Alister McGrath,

In contrast to Darwin's bleak final outlook, Christianity has at its roots a rich and vibrant doctrine of creation vitally connecting the created order with the Creator via the person and work of Jesus Christ. In addition, because Christianity also offers such a rich and full perspective on the value of the created order, life, and ultimate meaning, it therefore provides the richest foundation upon which to build an environmental ethic. By engaging the creation texts in Genesis 1 and 2, we can begin to see the beauty and wonder not only of what was created but, more foundationally, of the Creator himself and the value and purposes he imbued to the creation.

Genesis 1:1

The very first words of the Bible are typically rendered in English as "In the beginning God created the heavens and the earth" (Gen 1:1).[6] While it may be tempting to focus one's reading on that which is created, it is crucial instead to recognize that the subject of the biblical creation narrative is God himself. Properly understood, the opening words of the Bible are meant not to rivet our attention on the created order, but on the Creator and his stunning power and grace displayed in his creating activity. After all, not only is he the One who created the "heavens and the earth," but as the Scripture elsewhere affirms, even the heavens he created "are telling of the glory of God" and its "expanse is declaring the work of His hands" (Ps 19:1). What the psalmist seemed to understand, and the first point that we must take great care to emphasize, is that while the creation itself is beautiful, its chief function is not to draw attention to its own beauty, but to draw attention instead to the wonder and glory of the One who created it.

Historically, the doctrine of the Trinity has been one of the most difficult to comprehend and articulate, yet one clearly taught in the Bible. When we speak of the triune nature of God, we understand that there are three distinct persons who share one essence—one *homoousion*. Both the Old and New Testaments make plain the idea that creation is a work of the whole Godhead. The three persons of the Trinity perform the creative work together in perfect harmony and communion. As Wayne Grudem puts it, "God the Father was the primary agent in initiating the act of

---

The Reenchantment of Nature: The Denial of Religion and the Ecological Crisis (New York: Doubleday, 2002), 59.

6. Hebrew: *Bereshit bara Elohim et hashamayim ve'et ha'arets.*

creation. But the Son and the Holy Spirit were also active."[7] Thus, the ministry of the Father does not preclude that of the Son or the Spirit or vice versa.

Specifically, regarding the Gen 1:1 text, the word used for God is *Elohim*. This word is a plural form of the word *El* from which we get the English word "God." Interestingly, we also see the word translated "to create" is *bara*, which is singular case. From the very first words of Scripture, then, we see not only an emphasis on God as Creator but an indication that this creator God is a plural being. In other words, from the beginning of the biblical narrative, we see clues that the creation was accomplished by the triune God.[8]

Indeed, while all three persons of the Godhead are involved in the creation process, Scripture itself reveals that among the three persons of the Trinity, it is the Second Person—Jesus Christ—who is the primary agent of creation order.[9] For example, 1 Cor 8:6 clearly teaches that God is the source of all things, but it is through Christ's agency that all things have been created:

> Yet for us there is but one God, the Father, from whom are all things, and we exist for Him; and one Lord, Jesus Christ, by whom are all things, and we exist through Him.

Likewise, the first words in the Gospel of John echo Gen 1:1 in emphasizing the central role of God in creation but specifying the agency of Jesus Christ, the Word, in creation:

> In the beginning was the Word, and the Word was with God, and the Word was God. He was in the beginning with God. All things came into being by Him, and apart from Him nothing came into being that has come into being. (John 1:1–3)

In the words of Danny Akin, "John's Logos is a person. John's Logos is not only God's agent in creation; he is God."[10]

John Feinberg adds that "through Christ all things were made (John 1:3), and lest there be any doubts about what this means, the Gospel

7. Wayne Grudem, *Systematic Theology* (Grand Rapids, MI: Zondervan, 1994), 266.

8. We recognize at this point that our discussion of the Hebrew is clearly coming from a Christian perspective. That is, our modifying hermeneutic here is a reading of Gen 1:1 in light of the New Testament passages in John 1:1–12 and Col 1:15–20.

9. Grudem, *Systematic Theology*, 266.

10. Danny Akin, "The Person of Christ," in *A Theology for the Church*, ed. Danny Akin (Nashville: B&H, 2007), 493.

of John adds that nothing created was made through any agency other than Christ's. In verse 10, John repeats that the incarnate ('in the world') Christ made the world, even though the world didn't recognize him as creator or understand why he came."[11]

Colossians 1:16 also gives a very clear and affirming recognition of Christ as the creator of all things.

> For by Him all things were created, both in the heavens and on earth, visible and invisible, whether thrones or dominions or rulers or authorities—all things have been created by Him and for Him. (Col 1:16)

In this text, Paul very specifically identifies Jesus Christ, the Second Person of the Trinity, as the one who created "all things." Paul leaves little room for speculation regarding what this means as he gives exhaustive categories of what is included in "all things": *everything* in heaven and on earth; *everything* visible and invisible. In case there is any doubt about the supremacy of Christ in creation, Paul repeats in a summary statement the fact that "all things" are created by and for Christ. Danny Akin explains:

> Christ is the source-agent and preserver of creation and is worthy of all honor. It is Christ as sustainer ("by Him all things hold together") who makes the universe a cosmos instead of a chaos. A rare word in the New Testament, *prototokos* is used twice here because of its emphasis on the divine preeminence of Jesus as the Lord of his universal creation and his new creation, the church. Paul's point is that Christ is the Creator.[12]

Yet the Son does not create apart from the Father and the Holy Spirit. This is the essence of what *homoousion* means: three distinct persons, one God. Jesus fully shares the one and same divine essence with the Father and with the Holy Spirit. Thus, when dealing with the Genesis narrative, we must try to keep in mind that all things that the text reveals regarding the creation of heavens and earth are chiefly done through the ministry of Jesus. Lest we fall prey to some form of heretical modalistic thought, we recognize that all the qualities of the Godhead are fully present in Christ Jesus as he does his creative work.

God is the ground of all being and distinct from creation. One of the most fundamental elements to draw out of these texts is the fact that God is the ontological ground of all things that exist. That is, everything that

---

11. John S. Feinberg, *No One Like Him: The Doctrine of God* (Wheaton, IL: Crossway, 2001), 563.

12. Akin, "The Person of Christ," 503.

exists in the created realm does so because he gives it life and/or being. Nothing other than God existed prior to his creating and giving all things their existence. In his extensive work on the doctrine of God, John Feinberg helpfully points out that the phrase "in the beginning" provides the reference point for understanding how God created the heavens and the earth. This phrase in the Hebrew sentence structure sets forth an absolute sense of beginning in which nothing existed prior to creation but God alone. Thus, it has been the historical teaching of the church that God created *ex nihilo*—out of nothing—and passages such as Ps 33:6–9; John 1:3; Acts 4:24; Rom 4:17; Col 1:16; and Rev 4:11 all support the reality that God as an eternal being created all things and that all things have their beginning in Jesus Christ's creative activity.[13] Hebrews 11:3 certainly affirms this historically orthodox notion by unequivocally stating that "the worlds were prepared by the word of God, so that what is seen was not made out of things which are visible."

Recalling the words of Col 1:16 (indicating that all things were created *by* him and *for* him), we understand that Scripture establishes the fact that we are utterly dependent upon Christ for both our existence and our direction and purpose. Simply put, if God, through the agency of the person of Jesus Christ, had not chosen to create and bring all things that exist into existence, nothing else would exist (John 1:1–13) and obviously any questions about purpose or direction would be irrelevant.

Further, not only is the created realm utterly dependent upon God for its existence and ordering, it is also clearly distinct in nature from God. That is, while creation depends on him, it is in no way proper to suggest that God *is* nature or that the created realm is somehow of divine essence. Once again Feinberg's thoughts are helpful when he writes that "Unlike views of that day which deified things in the natural order, and unlike the later views that would be pantheistic, Genesis makes a radical distinction between the being and power of the creator and the creature. . . . God is immanent in his creation not because the creature is divine but because the creator God longs to commune and fellowship with his creatures . . . ontologically, [however], he thoroughly transcends all that is."[14] Henri Blocher makes a similar point in his study entitled "God and the Cross" when he comments that the world is "totally dependent on God's will and power yet distinct from God; God is the only *arche*

---

13. Feinberg, *No One Like Him*, 552–57. See also David P. Nelson, "The Work of God: Creation and Providence," in *A Theology for the Church*, ed. Danny Akin (Nashville: B&H, 2007), 250–60.

14. Feinberg, *No One Like Him*, 573.

[beginning or first principle] of the world and yet distinct and independent from it."[15]

This is an important point to ponder for a few moments because there has been such a tendency to suggest that those who are greatly concerned about the environment—including evangelicals—are somehow in danger of slipping into a pantheistic view of the universe. This certainly need not be the case. As John Frame rightly puts it, the doctrine of creation as we see it here revealed in Gen 1:1, "denies pantheism or monism, the view that creation is made of God's own being, a kind of emanation from him, as light from the sun, so that the creation itself is divine."[16] Simply put, Scripture is clear on this point, and in a carefully developed Christ-centered ethic, any suggestion of pantheism or monism must be utterly rejected.[17]

The contingent nature of creation's being and purpose. Because, as Gen 1:1 indicates, the Creator is ontologically transcendent above the created realm and stands in contradistinction from it in terms of its nature and essence, we understand that all of creation (humans included) are *contingent* beings. That is, our existence—and the existence of the entire universe—is impossible without the prior existence of One who created us. It follows from this, and specifically from the words of Col 1:16, that not only is our being contingent, so also is our meaning. Contrary to the popular myth of Enlightenment modernity and now postmodernity, human beings are not autonomous, nor is human purpose and meaning limited to that which is found in their habituated communities. Rather, each of us, and nature as a whole, has been given an inherent purpose by the creator Jesus Christ. If it is true that we and all of creation are not here of our own accord, if we are not autonomous, if someone put us here, then it is only logical to assume that he put us here for a purpose—a purpose that is bigger than ourselves. Certainly, this is the affirmation of Col 1:16 when it says that we were created by him and *for* him.

III. The Inherent Value of the Creation

So what is the purpose we were created for? Thomas Aquinas once wrote that knowing the purpose of creation can be discovered by recognizing

---

15. Henri A. Blocher, "God and the Cross," in *Engaging the Doctrine of God: Contemporary Protestant Perspectives*, ed. Bruce L. McCormack (Grand Rapids, MI: Baker, 2008), 137.

16. John Frame, *The Doctrine of God* (Phillipsburg, NJ: P&R, 2002), 299.

17. For a further discussion of why Pantheism must be rejected from a Christian point of view, see Schaeffer, *Pollution*, 15–35.

"the very dependency of the created act of being upon the principle for which it is produced."[18] What Aquinas was driving at is the idea that everything that exists does so not only on the basis of God's creative work and power but also by and for the purposes he gives to them. Therefore, it follows that the existence of a thing will reach its highest and fullest expression of itself *as it adheres to the reason for which it was created.*[19]

This is why when Col 1:16 instructs us that all things are not only created by Christ but also *for* Christ, it is of utmost importance for our lives and ethics that we discover what the purpose of Christ is for all of creation and then to live according to it. In other words, in keeping with our primary metaphor, if Jesus is *True North*, then it is only by orienting our entire lives toward following his purposes that we will live the life we were created to live. Knowledge of his purposes would function as the moral compass by which to navigate our lives.

Further, this is also why it is so important to understand that the primary subject of Gen 1:1 is God himself. Understanding the purpose of creation and the human's role in it begins with the recognition that the creation passages are meant to focus our attention preeminently on God as the primary source and goal of all things. This, of course, does not denigrate in any way the importance of the creation, but rather puts it into context. Over and over again in the Genesis 1 creation account, the text indicates that it is God who is doing the creating and it is God who is judging the value of the creation. He is preeminent and supreme over it all. Thus, the beauty of the masterpiece is meant to stir wonder over the Master who created it. The function and use of the masterpiece is meant to be in accord with the Master's created purposes. It was created *by* him and *for* him.

Alister McGrath captures this idea beautifully in his book *The Reenchantment of Nature* when he writes,

> Nature can thus be viewed or "seen as" . . . the work of a master craftsman, and the wisdom of the creator can thus be seen in the ordering of the world, in much the same way as the wisdom of an architect can be seen in the design of a great building. Creation is thus about imposing structure upon reality—a structure that the human mind can subsequently perceive and grasp. . . . As the French Renaissance thinker

---

18. Thomas Aquinas, *Summa Contra Gentiles* 2.18.2.
19. Its being or fundamental existence rests upon the fact that it has been given being by God. Being does not diminish when a person or thing is not aligned with its final purpose. However, the quality of the existence *is* dependent largely upon its alignment with its created design and purpose.

Jean Bodin (1539–96) put it in his *Universae naturae theatrum* (The Theater of the Universe of Nature): "We have come into this theater of the world for no other reason than to understand the admirable power, goodness and wisdom of the most excellent creator of all things, to the extent that this is possible, by contemplating the appearance of the universe and all his actions and individual works, and thus to be swept away more ardently in praise of him."[20]

The Goodness of Creation

The Christian doctrine of creation affirms that the created order has its own being—albeit contingent—and thus it also has an inherent value given by God. This inherent goodness of the created order is clearly established and emphatically pronounced by God in the Genesis 1 text. Six times the creation narrative declares that God "saw" that what he had made was "good"—prior to the creation of human beings (1:4,10,12,18,21,25). This goodness was not only a reality flowing from the declaration of the Lord, but as the text clearly indicates, it was also something he observed. Therefore, the goodness of creation—by God's design and grace—is inherent within it. Please note, this does not mean that creation is independent of God or functions autonomously from God. No, as Col 1:17 indicates, it is in Christ that all things in the created realm "hold together." But, having once again recognized the contingent nature of creation, we also recognize creation's inherent value given by God's creative grace.

It is important, here, to re-emphasize that God made six declarations that his created order was "good" prior to the creation of human beings. This reality points us directly to the fact that the created order has within it an inherent or intrinsic goodness *apart from the instrumental value* it plays in the life and existence of human beings. Therefore, as Christopher Wright explains, we can assert that

> the goodness of creation is of the essence of creation itself. It is not contingent on our human presence within it and our ability to observe it. In the creation narratives, the affirmation of "It is good" was not made by Adam and Eve but by God himself. So the goodness of creation (which includes its beauty) is theologically and chronologically prior to

---

20. McGrath, *The Reenchantment of Nature*, 11–12.

human observation. It is something that *God* saw and affirmed before humanity was around to see it.[21]

This point seems only to be affirmed when one considers the beautiful and poetic expression of Psalm 104, which first establishes the fact that God is the centerpiece of the story and then goes on to marvel at how God created everything as beautiful apart from (but not opposed to) its service to humanity.

> The high mountains are for the wild goats; the cliffs are a refuge for the seraphanim. He made the moon for the seasons; the sun knows the place of its setting. You appoint darkness and it become night, in which all the beasts of the forest prowl about. The young lions roar after their prey and seek their food from God. . . . O Lord, how many are Your works! In wisdom You have made them all; the earth is full of Your possessions. . . . Let the glory of the Lord endure forever; let the Lord be glad in His works. (Ps 104:18–31)

Walter Harrison writes of this psalm, "I know of no more direct word in the Bible about the independent significance of things and creatures on which man does not depend for life. The creative and powerful anthropo-centrism of biblical religion is here beautifully qualified: God has interest in badgers and wild goats and storks for their own sakes. He has interest in trees and mountains and rock-cairns that simply serve *non-human purposes*."[22]

A similar point emerges from meditation on Psalm 29. Here David celebrates the work of God by virtually ignoring the instrumental value that nature might have for man. Instead, the creation is celebrated in its own right as a depiction of the glory and strength of the Lord and the praise he is due. "Here as elsewhere the biblical writers presuppose that God has a relation to nature distinct from his intimate relation to man, that nature has worth to God apart from its role in the Divine-human drama."[23]

The point deserves emphasis: Scripture clearly indicates that creation—as creation—does indeed have an inherent value and beauty that is not

---

21. Christopher J. H. Wright, *The Mission of God: Unlocking the Bible's Grand Narrative* (Downers Grove, IL: InterVarsity, 2006), 398.

22. Walter Harrelson, "On God's Care for the Earth: Psalm 104," *Currents in Theology and Mission* 2 (1975): 20–21 (emphasis mine), quoted in Wright, *The Mission of God*, 399–400.

23. H. Paul Santmire, *Brother Earth: Nature, God, and Ecology in a Time of Crisis* (Nashville: Thomas Nelson, 1970), 85.

contingent upon its usefulness to human beings. It is inherently valuable and beautiful in its own right—because that is the way God made it and treats it. "God values the earth because he made it and he owns it."[24]

Now obviously, if one is not careful to place this value and beauty in proper context and see all these things via a larger view of the purposes and mission of God, then it is easily conceivable that an inferior perspective in which nature is appreciated without reference to God could come to dominate. However, ultimately we think McGrath captures the point well when he writes, "The dangers of allowing the beauty of the world to displace the prior and superior beauty of God must be noted, and allowed their proper place in Christian reflection on nature. Yet they in no way detract from the immense significance with which they invest the natural order."[25] Therefore, it seems that when considering the inherent value of the created realm, one must be careful of two things. First, we must be careful not to get sidetracked from the *True North* orientation of giving God ultimate glory because of the beauty found throughout the created realm. Second, we also must not miss the scripturally revealed fact that God's created realm has a value and beauty independent of an instrumental worth to human beings. God made all things, and thus, they have an inherent God-derived value and beauty in their own right.

Perhaps this is why God points out that the created order is not merely matter that exists to be exploited. No, as Ps 24:1 so clearly reminds us, "the earth is the Lord's and all it contains." Deuteronomy 10:14 makes the same point clear by emphatically declaring: "Behold, to the LORD your God belong heaven and the highest heavens, the earth and all that is in it." God owns it all. The entirety of creation belongs to God. God greatly values what he owns.

The Joy of God

One of the sweetest wonders that emerges when one studies the Scriptures and sees how God describes his created realm is the recognition that he takes joy in what he has made. Scripture indicates that not only does God create nature with its own inherent value, "God also is depicted as creating nature for the sake of his own enjoyment. . . . This is part of the significance of the expression, 'And God saw that it was good.'"[26] In other words, God's repetitive declaration that creation is "good" not only

---

24. Wright, *The Mission of God*, 399.
25. McGrath, *The Reenchantment of Nature*, 19.
26. Santmire, *Brother Earth*, 83.

indicates inherent value, but also hints toward the pleasure God takes in his own creative work and his approval of it.[27]

Psalm 104:26, in particular, is very interesting in this regard. In this passage that depicts the Lord's care over all his works, the psalmist indicates that in forming the sea, God also formed "leviathan" to "sport" or "play" therein. Thus, we discover that in creating the earth God's interaction with it appears to have an inherent element of "joy" that is exhibited when his creations express their being and function in accordance with their nature as well as in alignment with the purposes for which he created them.

Expanding on this point, Paul Santmire comments, "We might venture to render this thought in modern idiom by saying that God created the extra-galactic nebulae to play with them."[28] Indeed, it would seem that in clothing and arraying the flowers of the fields in such a beautiful manner (Matt 6:28–30), God gave to the flowers an inherent value and beauty (they are "good"; cf. Gen 1:12) that he finds pleasurable. Certainly this truth would later be identified by Jesus to teach his disciples about God's provision and love for them. More than mere instrumental value, Jesus recognized an inherent beauty in the flowers that he assumed all could see and appreciate. By the mere fact that they exist with recognizable beauty, they bring praise to God and he finds pleasure in them.

If the flowers can bring glory and pleasure to God by simply being what they are created to be, ought not humans and the entirety of creation together bring glory and joy to God as they exist and function in alignment with their created purposes? Certainly human beings are told they can enter into the joy of their Master (Matt 25:21). Perhaps, then, it is not a long stretch to recognize that the nonhuman created order might also bring a lesser but very real joy to the Master.

Valuing What God Values

The reality that God made the earth, owns the earth, and declares that it is "good" surely leads us to an important point of perspective and application. As Richard Young puts it so well, because of the inherent value in the created order itself—a value imbued to it by its Creator—"the object of our love is not only God and fellow humans, but everything God loves, that is, His entire creation. If one does not love nature, the

---

27. Millard Erickson, "Biblical Theology of Ecology," in *The Earth Is the Lord's: Christians and the Environment*, ed. Richard D. Land and Louis A. Moore (Nashville: Broadman, 1992), 44.

28. Santmire, *Brother Earth*, 84.

love cannot be called divine love, for it would be selective and partial."[29] Therefore we believe we are on solid ground theologically to affirm that it is good and right not only to recognize the high value God places on nature for its own right but also as those striving to be imitators of Christ in character and deed, Christians must learn to conform their loves and tastes to that which God himself highly values. In his book *Our Father's World*, Ed Brown captures the idea in the following manner:

> My biggest reason for caring for God's creation has nothing to do with the extent or the severity of the crisis, the number of people affected, or even the ultimate future of the human race. It has to do with one simple fact: I know the God who made it all. And I love him. If I can place a high price on things that have little or no intrinsic value simply because they were made by one of my children, how much more ought I to value and care for this amazing world God made, this world that is precious because he made it and that represents an excellence and beauty far beyond anything that any of us could begin to comprehend, let alone make on our own.[30]

Going even further on this point, if one simply remembers that human beings are a part of the created order (something we will discuss more fully in the following chapter), then it is not hard at all to see how it is possible to love the creation as God loves it. Of course, we are not extending the value of personhood to the nonpersonal beings and elements, but simply recognizing the point that in loving human beings we are loving a significant part of the created order. There is nothing inherently wrong in loving that which God loves in the created order.

Appreciating the value of this point, however, we believe it crucial and wise once again to explicitly make a distinction here for the sake of clarity. Highly esteeming nature should in no way be confused with some type of worship of nature or deification of nature. As we affirmed earlier in this chapter,

> the Bible makes a clear distinction between God the Creator and all things created. . . . Nothing in creation is in itself divine. . . . The Hebrew Bible, therefore, while it certainly teaches respect and care for the nonhuman creation, resists and reverses the human tendency to

29. Richard A. Young, *Healing the Earth: A Theocentric Perspective on Environmental Problems and Their Solutions* (Nashville, TN: B&H, 1994), 212.

30. Edward R. Brown, *Our Father's World: Mobilizing the Church to Care for Creation* (Downers Grove, IL: InterVarsity, 2006), 43.

divinize or personalize the natural order, or to imbue it with any power independent of its personal Creator.[31]

In showing a loving care for the creation, then, the Christian is to steer his love for creation toward a higher and more perfect love of the Savior. Likewise, that is where he ought always to point all others who love and esteem the natural order. Clearly there is a principle of transference of love from lesser to greater and a reciprocal expectation of love for greater toward lesser. Put in simpler terms, *in loving or esteeming the creation, let it drive you to loving and esteeming the Creator; in loving and esteeming the Creator, recognize the inherent beauty and value of his creation—value the creation as God values it.*

There is no question that sometimes this distinction is not clearly made, and some can find themselves walking too closely to (and perhaps stepping over) the line between love and worship. Tony Campolo recognized this tendency when he pointed out that "there really is a tendency for many Christians, who become 'green' in their activism and commit themselves to making environmental issues a vital part of their faith, to also become seriously confused in their thinking. I must be ready to admit that there really is some truth to the accusation that some green Christians end up talking very much like New Agers and in time end up espousing some New Age theology."[32] Once again we point out McGrath's comments along the same lines, that "the dangers of allowing the beauty of the world to displace the prior and superior beauty of God must be noted, and allowed their proper place in Christian reflection on nature."[33]

Having made this point, McGrath goes on to properly avoid overreaction to this tendency by qualifying that this danger should "in no way detract from the immense significance with which [the beautiful things God has created] invest the natural order."[34] In other words, we must not throw the proverbial baby out with the bathwater. Just because some get confused does not mean we should be afraid of valuing creation as God values it! Based on the manner in which Scripture reveals God's passionate concern for his created order, we can rightly say, then, that highly esteeming nature and nature's beauty—and being concerned to

---

31. Wright, *The Mission of God*, 400.

32. Tony Campolo, *How to Rescue the Earth Without Worshipping Nature: A Christian's Call to Save Creation* (Waco, TX: Word, 1992), 4.

33. McGrath, *The Reenchantment of Nature*, 19.

34. Ibid.

care for it—is right and proper.[35] We simply must also note and be on guard against the tendency of the human heart to wander and make idols out of things God never intended us to worship (see Romans 1).

On the other hand, however, we must also be careful not to denigrate or neglect what God declares wondrous simply out of fear and overreaction. Such a choice would indicate immaturity and theological shallowness. Thus, while on the one hand we must reject a worship of nature, on the other we must also reject an underappreciation and lack of care for it. Christopher Wright is correct to point out that "our treatment of the earth reflects our attitude to its Maker and the seriousness (or otherwise) with which we take what he has said about it."[36] We must, therefore, seek both to stoke the fires of passion for God's creation as an act of worshipping the Creator, while at the same time guarding the idol factory that is the human heart from turning to lesser things and desecrating ourselves in the process.

IV. The Inherent Purpose of Creation

Nonhuman Creation's Inherent "Directional Vector"

While we have affirmed that creation does have an inherent value in itself, we now want to focus more directly on the clear teaching of Scripture that there is a divinely instituted role for creation in the mission of God that gives it a value far transcending its inherent worth. By its very design, its inherent nature, its exquisite beauty, and its wondrous splendor, the created realm reaches its highest value and most fulfilling role as it sings out the glory of God and brings him praise. We reiterate the focal point of Gen 1:1 and proclaim along with David in Ps 19:1 that "the heavens are telling of the glory of God; and their expanse is declaring the work of his hands." God is the ultimate end of all things, and all things

---

35. And it is at this point that one can find a basis for cobelligerence with those who ultimately do not share the same worldview regarding care for the environment. However, cobelligerence toward caring for the environment should never satisfy the believer, as his or her longing should ultimately be the same as that of creation itself: that all creation would find a ceasing to its groaning because it (and every person) is restored to a right relationship with the Creator. Evangelism, then, could be said to "trump" environmental concern, but in actuality it would be better to say that because all people are God's creation, evangelism must be seen as a core element of environmental concern and that creation care discussions should always seek—as nature itself does—to point all persons toward the person and glory of Christ.

36. Wright, *The Mission of God*, 398.

that are created are designed by God to point out the glory of God. We appreciate how McGrath makes the point here.

> The divine creation of the world establishes an analogy between the creator and what is created. The beauty of the world thus reflects the beauty of God. Nature is like a mirror, itself beautiful while reflecting an even greater beauty of God. To study the wonder of nature is to glimpse tantalizing facets of the face of God, and long to see more. . . . Something of the torrent of God's beauty can thus be known in the rivulets of the beauty of the creation. This has long been recognized as one of the most basic religious motivations for scientific research—the passionate belief that to gain an enhanced appreciation of the beauty of the world is to glimpse something of the glory of God.[37]

In this sense, the created order is to function as a sort of signpost directing all to orient themselves to *True North*—God himself and "the torrents of his beauty." All of creation has been designed by God not only to be a pointer—a beautiful pointer to be sure—but also to be a loudspeaker that by its very existence is designed to declare God's presence and awaken in us a longing to be rightly aligned with him and know him in ever-increasing ways.

This is the basic meaning of the universe. Any denial of it is an attempt to rob it of its most important element and will ultimately undercut the very foundation of environmental ethics itself. On the other hand, it is in recognition of this inherent purpose to glorify God that we can lay the basic foundation for a lasting creation-care movement.

---

37. McGrath, *The Reenchantment of Nature*, 16. McGrath cites Jonathan Edwards's personal reflections on this same theme in order to relate how beauty in creation is meant to point the observer, the lover of nature, to that which is higher than nature—God and his beautiful glory. He writes, "In his *Personal Narrative*, Edwards wrote of his 'sheer beholding of God's beauty' as he walked in the New Jersey countryside: 'As I was walking there and looking up into the sky and clouds, there came into my mind so sweet a sense of the glorious *majesty* and *grace* of God, that I know not how to express. I seemed to see them both in a sweet conjunction . . . it was a sweet and gentle holy majesty; and also a majestic meekness. . . .' Edwards writes thus of the transformation in perceptions resulting from seeing nature as God's creation: 'The appearance of everything was altered; there seemed to be, as it were, a calm sweet cast, or appearance of *divine glory, in almost every thing*. God's Excellency, his wisdom, his purity and love, seemed to appear in every thing; in sun, moon, and stars; in the clouds, and blue sky; in the grass, flowers, trees; in the water, and all nature; which used greatly to fix my mind. I often used to sit and view the moon for continuance; and in the day spent much time in viewing the clouds and sky, to behold the sweet glory of God in these things' in the meantime, singing forth with a low voice my contemplations of the Creator and Redeemer.' The perception of beauty that we experience 'when we are delighted with flowery meadows and gentle breezes' is, for Edwards, nothing other than an intimation of the beauty of God." See *The Reenchantment of Nature*, 13–14.

The Pattern of the Universe: *Exitus et Reditus*

Earlier in the chapter we pointed out that Scripture clearly identifies Jesus Christ as the agent of creation. Colossians 1:16–17 indicates that all things were created *by* him and *for* him, and it is in him that all things hold together. One can detect from this passage a basic pattern that underlies all of God's working and has for two millennia given shape to Christian ethics: exit and return.

> All things were created by him: exit.
> All things were created for him: return.

The triune God, who is in the beginning and has an eternally independent existence, speaks into existence all things other than himself that now exist. All things that exist are designed by their very nature to bring glory back to him. Exit from God and return to God (Latin: *exitus et reditus*).[38] When that which is created by Jesus Christ seeks to return all glory and honor in all things back to Jesus Christ, that element of creation can be said to have found *True North*. This fundamentally Christocentric foundation or pattern inherent within all aspects of creation in turn becomes the basis for understanding the very nature of all ethics in the created realm. Everything is created by him and for him (Col 1:17). Santmire captures this idea well when he writes:

> In the Bible, creation is not an isolated event or end in itself; it is a beginning which looks forward to the final goal of all things, the consummated Kingdom of God. The alpha has meaning, in other words, only insofar as it is directed toward the omega. Creation is not just "back there"; creation is this present world as it is determined by, and moving toward, the Final Future of God.[39]

Indeed, it should come as no surprise that as a means of building his case for Christian faith and life, the apostle Paul would engage in a theological discussion of the natural order of the universe in chaps. 1–3 of the book of Romans. He does this by pointing to the ingrained patterns of the created order that demonstrate that all human beings are responsible to align their lives to *True North*. As a result, this pattern has impact on human responsibility both through an external witness (Rom 1:20–23)

---

38. For a nice short discussion on this theological scheme, see Peter Kreeft's *Summa of the Summa* (San Francisco: Ignatius, 1990), 15.

39. Santmire, *Brother Earth*, 82.

and the internal witness of the conscience (Rom 1:19; 2:14–15).[40] In this manner, Paul clearly indicates a level of moral accountability present to human beings apart from the written laws of God but fundamentally present in all aspects of the created order. Indeed, St. Augustine would elaborate on this idea by describing human existence prior to the fall as a period in which image bearers lived in a sinless state harmonious with the laws of nature. He argued that the universe itself was so ordered and structured prior to the fall that humans had no need for a written law because the laws of God were not only present in the fabric of the universe—in nature—but also "imprinted on the heart of man as a seal upon wax."[41]

While both Paul and Augustine recognized that sin marred the ability of all creation to be rightly aligned with *True North* (a topic we will address in chap. 4), the engrained patterns of the universe and moral law were not effaced by sin and the fall. As Augustine put it, "iniquity itself does not efface" the laws that govern the created universe.[42] In other words, a person's ability to perceive and rightly interpret the fundamental patterns of the universe and any accompanying moral laws may diminish through sin, but this diminished capacity should not be equated with an actual loss of the pattern and moral fabric itself. In other words, my inability to see oxygen does not diminish the reality that oxygen exists. Thus, when God gives to humans the Scriptures in written form, it is not because the natural laws that are engrained in the basic fabric of the universe no longer exist; rather, he gives them because human ability to know and perceive them became damaged by the fall. Again, in Augustine's words, "God wrote on the tables of the Law what men did not read in their hearts."[43]

One need not look far into the Reformation tradition to see that the notion of an ingrained pattern and inherent structure present in the universe has a rich and honored place among its foremost thinkers. For example, Luther commented that

> Not an individual is there who does not realize, and who is not forced to confess, the justice and truth of the natural law outlined in the command, "All things therefore whatsoever ye would that men should do unto you, even so do ye also unto them." The light of this law shines in

40. For a fuller discussion here, see Mark D. Liederbach, "The Moral and Religious Conscience" (Ph.D. diss., University of Virginia, 2000).
41. Augustine, *De Trin.* 14, 15, 21. See also *De Lib. Arbit.* 16.
42. Augustine, *Conf.* 2, 4, 9.
43. Augustine, *En. in Ps.* 57, 1.

the inborn reason of all men. Did they but regard it, what need have they of books, teacher or laws? They carry with them in the depths of their hearts a living book, fitted to teach them fully what to do and what to omit, what to accept and what to reject, and what decision to make.[44]

Calvin likewise recognized the existence of this basic pattern knitted into the fabric of the universe when in the *Institutes* he writes:

It is a fact that the law of God which we call the moral law is nothing else than a testimony of natural law and of that conscience which God has engraved on the minds of men. Consequently, the entire scheme of this equity of which we are now speaking has been prescribed in it. Hence this equity alone must be the goal and rule and limit of all laws.[45]

In fact, the consistency among Reformers on their recognition of this basic moral pattern led John T. McNeill to comment:

There is no real discontinuity between the teaching of the Reformers and that of their predecessors with respect to natural law. Not one of the leaders of the Reformation assails the principle. Instead, with the possible exception of Zwingli, they all on occasion express a quite ungrudging respect for the moral law naturally implanted in the human heart and seek to inculcate this attitude in their readers. Natural law is not one of the issues on which they bring the Scholastics under criticism. With safeguards of their primary doctrines but without conscious resistance on their part, natural law enters into the framework of their thought and is an assumption of their political and social teaching. . . . For the Reformers, as for the Fathers, canonists, and the Scholastics, natural law stood affirmed on the pages of Scripture.[46]

How this theological understanding of the "natural law" relates to understanding the ingrained exit and return (*exitus et reditus*) pattern of the universe and *True North* is a crucial element for developing an ethic of creation care. Perhaps no one in history set forth a clearer systematic

---

44. Martin Luther, "Sermon for the Fourth Sunday after Epiphany: Rom. 13:8–10," in *The Sermons of Martin Luther*, ed. John Nicholas Lenker, 8 vols. (Grand Rapids, MI: Baker, 1983), 7:73.
45. John Calvin, *Institutes*, IV.20.16.
46. John T. McNeill, "Natural Law in the Teaching of the Reformers," *Journal of Religion* 168 (1946): 27.

explanation of it than Thomas Aquinas in his classic work *Summa Theologica*.

The Relationship of Natural Law to *Exitus et Reditus*

Thomas Aquinas taught that all of the laws and the fundamental moral structure of the universe are founded upon, and exist because of, the nature of the God who is the Ruler of the universe. He argued that all law and moral structure does not exist merely because God commands them to exist, but rather, that they flow out of the nature of God himself. That is, they are reflective of God's very own nature and plan.

Eternal law, then, is the name Aquinas gave to the law that is identical to the mind, will, and plan of God as understood in its fullness only by God himself. God's plans and purposes are eternal as he himself is. Thus, all that exists does so because it was created by God and reflects to some degree in its very essence the eternal law of God. William E. May helpfully explains that "Thomas taught that all creation—the cosmos and all things within it—is under the governance of God's intelligence. Thus, the eternal law is the *ratio* or divine plan of the governance of all things insofar as this *ratio* or divine plan exists within the mind of God himself as the ruler of the universe."[47] Therefore, the end, to which the eternal law points, is that which is the ultimate good (*summum bonum*) of all things and that which will bring about ultimate happiness.[48]

Regarding *natural law*, then, Aquinas argues that "it is evident that all things partake somewhat of eternal law in so far as, namely from its being imprinted on them, they derive their respective inclinations to their proper acts and ends."[49] Therefore, to the degree that human beings perceive elements or portions of the eternal law and/or act according to it, they are participating in it. Likewise, as the nonhuman creation—nature itself—partakes of and functions in accordance with the eternal law, it rightly displays the mind and heart of God. The natural law, then, not only helps to govern human morality but also serves as a design placed into the grain of the universe orienting all of creation toward *True North*.

Crucial to this discussion, we emphasize that this natural law is a *participation in* the eternal law, not the invention or assertion of an idea concocted by humans or somehow independent from God. For Aquinas, the

---

47. William E. May, *An Introduction to Moral Theology* (Huntington, IN: Our Sunday Visitor, 1991), 45.

48. Thomas Aquinas, *Summa Theologica* I–II.90.2.

49. Ibid., I–II.91.2.

ontology of all law and this ingrained *exitus et reditus* pattern is *directly dependent* upon the existence of God. Thus, as J. Budziszewski explains,

> To call these first principles part of revelation is not a euphemism, for they come from God; they are utterly dependent on his arrangements in creation. We know them for no other reasons than the divinely ordained design of the world, the divinely ordained design of the intellect, and the divinely ordained correspondence between them. Creation may be fallen, but it has not been destroyed; its instructions may be resisted, but they cannot be overthrown; the knowledge of them may be suppressed, but it cannot be abolished.[50]

This idea is what C. S. Lewis also described in the *Abolition of Man* as the deeper structures of nature. There exists, he rightly argues, deeper structures in the universe that are not created or merely asserted by humans but which have been put in place by God. They are then discovered by humans as they rightly perceive the created realm.[51] They are meant to point each of us and all of creation toward its highest end and purpose.

It is the presence of this *exitus et reditus* pattern of the universe that we believe makes focusing on creation care out of a motivation of crisis not wrong but ultimately *shallow*. By using this term "shallow," we do not want to be mistaken as saying that a recognition of a crisis situation is unimportant. Rather, by "shallow" we mean "insufficient" and "impotent" and possibly misdirected in regard to ultimate importance. For while it may be the case that concern for environmental degradations could stimulate or catalyze action, it will only be when we recognize the deeper patterns inherent in the very nature of all things that we will begin to see that *creation care is not merely a matter of temporal survival—it is a matter of properly ordered eternal worship.*

Long term (and for the purposes of character development and lasting change in perspective), we as a people and race must engage at the level of this "deep structure" within the created universe and seek to conform ourselves (body and soul) to this underlying reality and purpose for all things if we hope to make any real and lasting change in ourselves or in

---

50. J. Budziszewski, *Evangelicals in the Public Square* (Grand Rapids, MI: Baker, 2006), 33.

51. C. S. Lewis, *Abolition of Man* (San Francisco: HarperOne, 2001), 43. See a similar discussion in *Mere Christianity,* where he unfortunately uses the designation of Tao to describe creation order natural laws that govern the universe. For a related use of this concept of deep structures in ethics, see also Max L. Stackhouse, "deep structures of existence," in Max L. Stackhouse, "A Premature Postmodern," *First Things* 10/2000, accessed at http://www.firstthings.com/article/2007/01/a-premature-postmodern-4 7.1.2009.

our actions. The fundamental reality is that all things have been created by God (*exitus*) to bring him glory (*reditus*). Thus, aligning ourselves with this reality and treating the created order in a way that also aligns with it becomes the fundamental pattern by which humans beings can most effectively bring praise unto God. It is the path of the entire creation to *True North*.

We love how McGrath so eloquently captures this idea:

> This is why, then, while it is right for us to recognize the inherent value and beauty of the creation order in its own right, we also recognize that nature is not complete in itself. It points to something, intimating the presence or promise of something even more wonderful. To study and understand nature is an excellent thing; to appreciate that something else lies beyond it does not in any way diminish the quality of the human engagement with nature in poetry, art, or science; if anything, it heightens the motivation for that quest. The greater our appreciation of the glory of nature, the greater our longing for a transcendent glory that lies beyond it but that is faintly reflected in our own world of experience. . . . Nature points upward, aesthetically and ontologically, and we fail to appreciate its richness until we become caught up in this *upward trajectory*. To observe the stars of the heavens is one thing; to see them as signs of a beauty and goodness that is yet to be fully revealed—but that we may anticipate now—is quite another.[52]

V. Conclusion

What we hope to have demonstrated in this chapter is that Genesis 1 indicates that "creation is an act of God alone, by which, for his own glory, he brings into existence everything in the universe, things that have no existence prior to his creative word."[53] In doing so, while God did desire that human beings would appreciate and love his creation, ultimately he wanted them and all of the created realm to recognize that he is the pinnacle of beauty and wonder, and all attention ultimately must find its source and fulfillment in him. Through the direct agency of Jesus Christ, the created order was given its essence and shape and purpose. To that end, John Jefferson Davis rightly asserts:

---

52. McGrath, *The Reenchantment of Nature*, 141; emphasis mine.
53. Frame, *The Doctrine of God*, 291.

Christ is the telos or final purpose for which all things exist, since all things were created not only by him but for him [Col 1:16b]. Consequently, no plant, animal, tree, forest, or ecosystem can be rightly viewed only in terms of its utilitarian value for man, but should be seen by the Christian in terms of its final purpose to reveal the glory and excellence of the one who created it.[54]

Foundationally, then, from a Christocentric perspective, an ethic of creation care must flatly reject as inadequate any notion of environmental concern that does not recognize the final ordering of all things toward God in Christ. Christ himself is the alpha and omega of all the universe. He himself is the center of the story. The primary question of Christian ethics, from this point of view, then, is how ought we best conform our lives and then direct all of creation toward this *True North* so that all things that live and move and have their being in Christ will return to him the glory that he is due because they were created *by* him and *for* him (Col 1:16).

At the conclusion of this chapter we simply reiterate that the fundamental pattern and purpose of the universe is that all things find their source and being in God; they are created by him according to his divine will and purposes; and they are meant to point back to him so that all of the created realm will give him glory. This is *True North*.

The specific and unique role that humans are to play in this journey of all creation toward *True North* is the subject to which we now turn.

---

54. John Jefferson Davis, *Evangelical Ethics: Issues Facing the Church Today*, 3rd ed. (Phillipsburg, NJ: P&R, 2004), 272.

3

Christ the Creator and Humanity's Unique Role in Creation

Strange are the ways of men, Legolas! Here they have one of the marvels of the Northern World, and what do they say of it? Caves, they say! Caves. . . . My good Legolas, do you know that the caverns of Helm's Deep are vast and beautiful? . . . No dwarf could be unmoved by such loveliness. . . . We would tend these glades of flowering stone, not quarry them. With cautious skill, tap by tap—a small chip of rock and no more, perhaps, in a whole anxious day—so we could work, and as the years went by, we should open up new ways, and display far chambers that are still dark, glimpsed only as a void beyond fissures in the rock. And lights, Legolas! We should make lights . . . and when we wished we would drive away the night that has lain there since the hills were made; and when we desired rest, we would let the night return.

Gimli, son of Gloin, in J. R. R. Tolkien's *The Lord of the Rings: The Two Towers*, 2nd ed. (Boston: Houghton Mifflin, 1965), 152–53

I. Introduction: Review and Outline

I n the previous chapter we began an interactive discussion with the Genesis narratives of creation in order to work toward building a biblical/theological foundation for an ethic of creation care. We presented the idea that foundational to any work in Christian ethics, one must begin with a focus on God and his character and actions. In regard to Christian environmental ethic, special attention needed to be paid to Christ as the Creator since Scripture identifies the Second Person of the Trinity as the primary agent of creation. As such, Christ is not only the One who creates the universe but in doing so he imparts a value to the created order that is inherent to it even though the creation itself is contingent upon God for its being, value, and purpose.

Further, we explored the idea that not only was everything created by Christ, it was also created for Christ. Thus, the directional purpose of the universe is that all things are created by God for the purpose of bringing him glory. That is, the motive for pursuing *True North* is for all things created to bring all the praise and glory to God that he is due. Specifically in regard to creation care, what this means is that Christian environmental ethics are not to be motivated or based on concerns of crisis or environmental degradations (although such concerns can catalyze action), but on the basis of the divine intent for creation. Any conflict of interests that may exist regarding the use of nature ultimately must be resolved in view of God's purposes for creation rather than mere human interests or concerns.[1]

In this chapter we want to continue this discussion of the Genesis 1 and 2 narratives, giving specific attention to the creation of human beings and how their unique purpose and role in the created order is related to the supremacy of Christ in all things and the orientation toward *True North* inherent in the nature of all things created. It is our contention here that not only are human beings created unique among all the visible created order as image bearers, but based on this grace they also have a unique role in bringing God glory and to maximizing the praise and glory of God throughout the entire created realm. The manner in which they are to go about accomplishing this task is through "subduing" and "ruling" in worshipful obedience. In this manner, then, not only will humans facilitate the quest for their own personal fulfillment and flourishing, but they will also facilitate the fulfillment and flourishing of all things created.

II. The Unique Place and Responsibility of Humans Among Creation

The Genesis accounts of creation contain three vitally important passages regarding the nature of human beings that we will focus on and develop in this chapter. The first, Gen 1:26–27, indicates that human beings are uniquely created by God as his image bearers. The second, Gen 2:15, discloses God's calling and directive purpose for Adam and all subsequent human beings. Third, Gen 1:28, gives descriptive content

---

1. Richard A. Young, *Healing the Earth: A Theocentric Perspective on Environmental Problems* (Nashville: B&H, 1994), 235.

to how God's image bearers are to function in the created order. We will develop each of these points in turn.

Genesis 1:26–27—Human Beings as Image Bearers (Gen 5:1; 9:6; 1 Cor 11:7; Jas 3:9)

> The God said, "Let Us make man in Our image, according to Our likeness; and let them rule over the fish of the sea and over the birds of the sky and over the cattle and over all the earth, and over every creeping things that creeps on the earth." God created man in His own image, in the image of God He created him; male and female He created them. (Gen 1:26–27)

This passage of Scripture is clearly God's statement of intentionality. It indicates without equivocation that God made a clear and forthright decision to create humanity. As with the rest of creation, God did not leave the process up to chance. Rather, by his wisdom and through his creative grace he fashioned two human beings exactly as he desired: image bearers who reflect his glory equally but distinctly via the two genders of male and female.

The statement that God created humans in his image establishes the fact that among all the creatures fashioned by God, there are none who hold a place of such high dignity as that enjoyed by the human race alone. Surely this is a wondrous thing to be given this privileged status. For as J. I. Packer says, being "image bearers" means at least in part that humans are to "act as his direct representatives on earth."[2] Grudem agrees when he writes, "the fact that man is in the image of God means that man is like God and represents God."[3] Grudem goes on to point out that

> Both the Hebrew word for "image" (*tselem*) and the Hebrew word for "likeness" (*demut*) refer to something that is *similar* but not identical to the thing it represents the "image" of. The word *image* can also be used of something that *represents* something else. . . . When we realize that the Hebrew words for "image" and "likeness" simply informed the original readers that man was *like* God, and would in many ways *represent* God, much of the controversy over the meaning of "image of God" is seen to be a search for too narrow and too specific a meaning. When

---

2. J. I. Packer, *Concise Theology: A Guide to Historic Christian Beliefs* (Wheaton, IL: Tyndale, 1993), 71.
3. Wayne Grudem, *Systematic Theology* (Grand Rapids, MI: Zondervan, 1994), 442.

Scripture reports that God said, "Let us make man in our image, after our likeness" (Gen 1:26), it simply would have meant to the original readers, "Let us make man to be *like* us and to *represent* us."[4]

Recognizing this vital element of human nature is crucial to our discussion on creation care because of the special place humans are granted within the created order. As Erickson points out, this image-bearing status and representative role is the essential element in understanding what a human person is. That is, "the image of God is what makes man man."[5] Therefore, it is in the functioning and proper expression of the image that man will reach his highest end and flourish.

We want to be careful at this point to clarify that it is not through a person's functional ability that he or she finds his or her fundamental *value* before the Lord. No, that is found first of all in the fact that he or she has been given existence and being from God and then is further established by the fact that he or she is an image bearer. Once again, Erickson's work is helpful for us to make this point. He writes, "The image should be thought of as primarily substantive or structural. The image is something in the very nature of man, in the way in which he was made. It refers to something man *is* rather than something he *has* or *does*. By virtue of his being man, he is in the image of God; it is not dependent upon the presence of anything else."[6] Thus, regardless of how a person lives, regardless of his or her capacity to function mentally or physically, he or she has an inherent value and should be treated with utmost dignity and care even beyond that of the rest of the visible created realm. As John Hammett points out, practically speaking, "the image of God is the basis for human dignity."[7]

Our discussion at this junction, however, is not primarily about inherent value, but the fulfillment of created purpose and destiny of each person who is by definition an image bearer. God created each and every one of us to fulfill a definite purpose and a highest end. Only when each of us individually and all of us corporately pursue and live for that end will we truly flourish as God designed and desires for us.

Obviously this begs the question as to what our created purpose is as image bearers. It is to Gen 2:15 that we must turn to discover the answer.

---

4. Ibid., 442–43.

5. Millard Erickson, *Christian Theology* (Grand Rapids, MI: Baker, 1983), 496.

6. Ibid., 513.

7. John Hammett, "Human Nature," in *A Theology for the Church*, ed. Danny Akin (Nashville: B&H Academic, 2007), 381.

III. The Image Bearer's Inherent Purpose

Critique of "Eco-Evangelical Orthodoxy" Translation of Genesis 2:15

> Then the LORD God took the man and put him into the garden of Eden to cultivate it and to keep it.

As Gen 2:15 indicates, God gave Adam a very special vocation and directive purpose as an image bearer. After God created Adam from the dust of the earth and animated him (Gen 2:7), he placed Adam into Eden in order to do something. To discover what it is he purposed for Adam to accomplish, we need to explore the meaning of the two words translated from the original Hebrew into English as "cultivate" and "keep." Contrary to what may appear to be simple farming instructions in the English translations, the original Hebrew meanings of each word and the entire context of the passage point to a much richer meaning than might be apparent at first glance. Indeed, the interpretation and meaning of these words and this passage, it is safe to say, are universally recognized by those in the environmental-ethics discussion as hinge points upon which much of the Christian perspective on creation care turns.

One of the more prominent interpretations of these words and this verse is represented vigorously by several influential evangelical voices in the creation-care debate, including Calvin DeWitt, Stephen Bouma-Prediger, and Loren Wilkenson. In fact, within the realm of evangelical environmental ethics, it is safe to say that their perspective has been received so favorably among "green Christians" that we can label this view as the "eco-evangelical orthodox" interpretation of the passage. Understanding the key elements of this position revolves around the basic meaning of the Hebrew words *'abad* and *shamar*.

First of all, the Hebrew word for "cultivate" is *'abad*. In various translations of Gen 2:15, this word has been rendered as "cultivate," "tend," "till," "work," or "dress." The Hebrew word for "keep" is *shamar*. It has been rendered in various translations as "keep," "watch over," and "safeguard." While each of these words can have a particular technical meaning, the best way to render a word when seeking to translate it is to seek the best meaning as it is derived from both the context of the immediate passage and the general surrounding context of the narrative. Proper translation involves a technically accurate term that *also* appropriately fits the context of the entire passage.

In his treatment of this passage, the influential zoologist and professor of environmental studies, Calvin DeWitt, believes the most appropriate English translations for these words should be "serve and keep." As he puts it: "Gen 2:15 conveys a marvelous teaching. Adam is expected by God to serve the garden and to keep it." His choice to interpret *'abad* with the English word "serve" is based on his assertion that it is a "possible translation" and one that is often rendered from the same root word in the Old Testament depending on the context in which the word is found. Whether this particular context warrants the rendering of "service" he does not argue. However, having opted for this interpretation, he goes on to comment that "God expected Adam and his descendants to meet the needs of the garden of creation so that it would persist and flourish. . . . God also expected Adam and his descendants to keep the garden. The word for keep (*shamar*) is sometimes translated as 'guard,' 'safeguard,' 'take care of,' and 'look after.' *Shamar* indicates a loving, caring, sustaining kind of keeping."[8]

In a similar vein, Loren Wilkinson comments in regard to the interpretation of *'abad* and *shamar* that "the significant thing about both words is that they describe actions undertaken not primarily for the sake of the doer, but for the sake of the object of the action. The kind of tilling that is a service of the earth. The keeping of the garden is not just for human comfort, but is a kind of preservation."[9] Thus, for Wilkinson, as for DeWitt, because the verse tells us to cultivate and keep "*it*" (i.e., the garden), he contends that the primary beneficiary of the cultivation or service (*'abad*) and keeping (*shamar*) is to be the garden and not the man (Adam). Thus, because the immediate context of the verse is the garden, he argues that the action rendered has "it" as the primary focus. Based on this, he also prefers to interpret the phrase using the possible translation of "service" toward the earth.

---

8. Calvin B. DeWitt, *Earth-Wise: A Biblical Response to Environmental Issues*, 2nd ed. (Grand Rapids, MI: Faith Alive, 2005), 44. In Roger S. Gottlieb's *A Greener Faith*, DeWitt comments in a similar fashion: "Service by creation to people must be reciprocated with service back to creation. Stewardship does not allow taking without giving back. Instead, it returns creation's service with returned human service that is given in appreciation, gratitude, and care" (New York: Oxford University Press, 2006), 194.

9. Loren Wilkinson, Peter DeVos, and Calvin DeWitt, *Earthkeeping in the Nineties: Stewardship of Creation* (Grand Rapids, MI: Eerdmans, 1991), 209.

Stephen Bouma-Prediger, in his *For the Beauty of the Earth*, follows suit in his treatment of Gen 2:15. In fact, his rhetoric even amplifies the intensity of the significance of the point. He argues that

> Genesis 2:5 speaks of humans serving the earth. . . . And Genesis 2:15—the last part of which is painted on the door of every Chicago police car—defines the human calling in terms of service: We are to serve [*'abad*] and protect [*shamar*]. We are to serve and protect the garden that is creation—literally be a slave to the earth for its own good, as well as for our benefit.[10]

He reiterates this point by affirming that "Genesis 1:28 must be placed alongside Genesis 2:15, where we are told that God put the human in the garden 'to till and keep it.' To till [*'abad*] means to serve the earth for *its own sake*, and to keep [*shamar*] means to protect the earth as one caringly guards something valuable."[11] Thus, Bouma-Prediger echoes a similar perspective to DeWitt and Wilkinson in his interpretation of *'abad* as "service" but goes further in his argument that the "service" rendered to the earth has some benefit to the human caretaker, but should primarily benefit the earth. Indeed, more than mere voluntary service, Bouma-Prediger asserts a moral imperative in which humans are meant to "slave" for the earth "for its own sake."

In regard to Gen 2:15, we applaud the efforts of all three of these men to rightly show that human concern is not central to the passage. For, as we alluded to in the previous chapter and will discuss below, Christian theology has been accused of making the value and purpose of created order completely subservient to human interests. In each case, these men rightly show that the passage says that Adam is to cultivate and keep "it" (the garden) and thus they rightly shift the emphasis away from an anthropocentric (human-centered) perspective about creation.

While we affirm this element of their interpretation, with all due respect to these important and influential men, we believe that their rendering of the passage and application of it, while technically possible, does not adequately take into context the greater picture of what is taking place in Genesis 1 and 2. To put it simply, we would argue that while there is an element of service that should be rendered to the earth, the text is far richer than any of these treatments allows for because of the

---

10. Steven Bouma-Prediger, *For the Beauty of the Earth* (Grand Rapids, MI: Baker, 2002), 74.
11. Ibid., 154; emphasis mine.

greater context of worship in which the entire creation narrative falls. We are persuaded that they have not gone "the full nine yards" in the discussion. In order to understand the reason we come to this conclusion, we must delve a bit deeper in an analysis of the Hebrew words *'abad* and *shamar* and their context in light of both the particular verse as well as the larger Genesis 1 and 2 context.

In his *Healing the Earth*, Richard A. Young offers a much more in-depth study of the Hebrew and points out that there are several common meanings the word can take on depending on the grammatical structure of the sentence and the context of the surrounding text.[12] According to Young, the most common meanings of *'abad* in Scripture are:

1. to work, especially when there is no object (Exod 5:18);
2. to cultivate, when the object is the ground, vineyard, or the like (Gen 3:23; 4:2,12; Deut 28:39; Prov 12:11; 28:19);
3. to work for someone either as a servant or slave (Exod 21:2–6; 2 Sam 16:19);
4. to serve or worship a deity (Exod 3:12; Judg 2:11; Ps 100:2);
5. to serve in a place of worship (Num 4:37,41).

Likewise, with the Hebrew word *shamar* Young points out that this verb also has several possible meanings that are dependent upon the general context of the passages in which they fall. These possible meanings include:

1. to watch or guard something, such as sheep (1 Sam 17:20), an entrance (1 Kgs 14:27), or a captive (1 Kgs 20:39);
2. to protect from danger (Ps 121:7; Prov 6:24);
3. to save or retain something, such as food (Gen 41:35);
4. to do something carefully or attentively, such as observe God's laws or covenant (Exod 15:26; 19:5).[13]

Now in regard to the interpretation of these words, normally when the ground (garden, earth) is the object of the sentence in which the verb *'abad* is found, then the meaning would best be understood as "till" or "cultivate." Thus, it is understandable, seeing as how the immediate context of Gen 2:15 involves a garden, how many English translations will render the word *'abad* as "cultivate." However, because of the larger context of the Genesis 1 and 2 creation accounts, it is clear that God has an even larger agenda in mind for both Adam and the garden. Young alludes

---

12. Young, *Healing the Earth*, 163.
13. Ibid.

to this larger agenda in his discussion when he points out that God's concern is with Adam functioning as a "manager to help keep order and harmony in creation" in which the service rendered was not done merely for his own sustenance but is to be *rendered unto God*.[14]

We find that Young's work is helpful in that he does not rely merely on the technical possibilities of the words at issue; rather, he appropriately seeks to place his interpretive efforts within the context of the entire Genesis narrative. By doing so he rightly hints at the fact that the narrative context is pointing toward a much higher end than even "serving" the garden.

Our interest in pursuing this "higher end" and context of the Genesis narrative should not be misconstrued as demeaning the point of emphasis or the importance of the work DeWitt, Wilkinson, and Bouma-Prediger have added to the discussion. Clearly, there is a service being rendered by Adam as he cares for the garden. We are simply convinced that the text tells us far more. Thus, to argue as Bouma-Prediger does (and DeWitt implies) that the service is rendered to the garden "for its own sake" *runs the risk* of merely replacing an anthropocentric motive for creation care with a biocentric one. That is, replacing a man-centered ethic with an ethic that gives final consideration to creation care because the creation has an inherent value. We also believe such a perspective *runs the risk* of ultimately missing the powerfully motivating theocentric tenor to the entire discussion. To put it another way, caring for the earth by serving or slaving for it "for its own sake" *does* rightly capture the idea (as we argued in the previous chapter) that the created order has a God-given inherent worth. However, caring for the earth "for its own sake" can also imply that the final goal or *telos* of the service rendered finds its fulfillment in the flourishing of the garden. We believe that such a conclusion would be not only tragic but also close to idolatry because the focus falls short of the inherent *True North* pattern in which all things are created to bring God glory.

To be fair, we are certain that none of these men ultimately takes a biocentric position in their ethic. Indeed, their writing indicates that each expressly seeks to give God ultimate glory as they argue for creation care. Of this we have no doubt. At this point of exegesis, however, their interpretive work does not adequately take into account all that is taking place in the creation narrative, and thus their rendering of Gen 2:15 as "serving and protecting" the earth ultimately puts more emphasis on

---

14. Ibid.

the creation than is necessary and less on worshipping the creator than is warranted.[15]

Creation as Temple

How, then, should we understand the vocation and directive purpose that God assigns to Adam in Gen 2:15? To rightly capture the overall thrust, we must first recall that the opening words of the Bible shape the entire context of the creation narrative to be one ultimately concerned with the God who was "in the beginning" and who created everything. In addition, we recall that John 1:1–3; 1 Cor 8:6; and Col 1:16–17 identify Jesus Christ as the agent of creation. Not only is this true, but all things were created *for* Christ. As we saw in the previous chapter, then, all things created by Christ are designed and patterned to return to Christ all the glory He is due. This foundational reality leads John Frame to argue in his *The Doctrine of God* that the heavens and earth function, as it were, as a temple for the worship of God.[16] Isaiah 66:1 certainly supports such a perspective as God compares the created world to the temple of Israel:

> Thus says the LORD, "Heaven is My throne and the earth is My footstool. Where then is a house you could build for Me? And where is a place that I may rest?"[17]

Similarly, in his important work "Creation in the Image of the Glory-Spirit," Meredith G. Kline points out that the Genesis 1 and 2 narratives are heavily laden with language picturing the created order as a temple of worship for the King of the universe.[18] Jamieson, Fausset, and Brown specifically discuss Gen 2:15 from the point of view that the garden functioned as a sort of "whole life temple." They comment that Eden "was in fact a temple in which [Adam] worshipped God, and was daily employed in offering the sacrifices of thanksgiving and praise."[19] Greg Beale's work *Temple and Church's Mission* makes the same basic case that the picture of

---

15. Even with Young, however, while his final interpretive understanding of Gen 2:15 does rightly suggest that the service rendered ultimately is "unto the Lord," we believe he also ultimately underemphasizes the degree to which the larger overall context of the creation narratives and the extent to which a theocentric perspective ought to drive the interpretation and translation of Gen 2:15.

16. John Frame, *The Doctrine of God* (Phillipsburg, NJ: P&R, 2002), 291.

17. Consider also passages such as Pss 11:4; 93; 103:19; Isa 40:21–23.

18. Meredith G. Kline, "Creation in the Image of the Glory-Spirit," *Westminster Theological Journal* 39 (1977): 250–72. See also *Images of the Spirit* (Grand Rapids, MI: Baker, 1980), 20–26.

19. Robert Jamieson, A. R. Fausset, and David Brown, *Commentary Critical and Explanatory on*

Eden described in the creation narrative has strong theological ties with the Old Testament's description of the temple as well as the idea that the whole of creation as restored by Christ is to be understood as the dwelling place or tabernacle of God.[20] Old Testament scholar Christopher J. H. Wright also concurs with this basic perspective.[21]

Building on this idea, Noel Due, in his book *Created for Worship*, argues that a strong connection exists between Eden and Adam's role as the king-priest who was designed and created to rule and shepherd all of creation. He comments, "The whole of Eden was built for worship. Adam was created to be the great leader of the creation in its glorification of God, with Eden as the garden-sanctuary of his communion with the Creator."[22] He also comments that in interpreting the Genesis creation narratives

> we should see humanity as being brought into, and existing in, a matrix of worship. The primal couple did not exist for themselves, or by themselves, but they existed for God, at the head of creation yet to be brought into its full glory. We see that the primal couple was given a mandate, to "fill" the earth, and "subdue" it and "rule over" it (Gen 1:26f), and a task to "cultivate and keep" the Garden (Gen 2:15). To engage in such tasks and to fulfill the mandate was to be their expression of worship. Their communion with God, the joy of his nearer presence, the offering of praise and adoration to him, were not to be set in some compartmentalized fashion away from their daily activity, but the daily activity was their service to God.[23]

In light of this larger context that places the entire created order in the framework of worship, it is possible—indeed preferable—to give a fuller and more proper meaning to the Hebrew words *'abad* and *shamar* than merely "cultivate" and "keep" or even "serve" and "protect." Recall that Young's work, noted above, indicates that there are several possible technical meanings to these two words, including "worship" and "obey." The appropriate translation, then, relies on the given context in which the

---

the Whole Bible (Glasgow: William Collins, Queen's Printer, 1863), 2–3. Cited at http://bible.cc/genesis/2-15.htm

20. G. K. Beale, *The Temple and the Church's Mission: A Biblical Theology of the Dwelling Place of God* (Downers Grove, IL: InterVarsity, 2004).

21. Christopher J. H. Wright, *The Mission of God* (Downers Grove, IL: IVP Academic, 2006), 415.

22. Noel Due, *Created for Worship*, Mentor of Christian Focus Publications (Ross-shire, Scotland: Geanies House, Fern, 2005), 41–42.

23. Ibid., 40.

word falls. Thus, it should come as no surprise in light of the larger context of Genesis 1 and 2 that renowned Hebrew scholar Umberto Cassuto would make the case that while the English phrase "cultivate and keep" or even "serve and care for" may be technically accurate, the original language and context strongly suggest the idea that God placed Adam in the garden to *worship* and *obey*.[24]

Respected Old Testament scholar John Sailhamer agrees. He points out that this important element is often lost in translation from ancient Hebrew to modern English. Many English translations, he argues, overlook the "specific purpose for God's putting man in the garden. In most [English versions] man is 'put' in the garden 'to work it and take care of it.'" Sailhamer objects, however, and argues "a more suitable translation of the Hebrew . . . would be 'to worship and obey.'" That is, when reading Gen 2:15 from the perspective of the language and the given context, the passage indicates that "man is put in the garden to worship God and to obey him. Man's life in the garden was to be characterized by worship and obedience."[25]

Thus, it is the fourth possible rendering in the above lists given by Young regarding the possible meanings of *'abad* and *shamar* that most fully capture the full intention of creation accounts given in Genesis 1 and 2. Certainly Adam was to "cultivate and keep" the garden. Certainly Adam was to "serve and protect it." Ultimately, however, Adam's cultivation and service were to be ordered unto God as worship that he perfectly rendered in obedience in light of the very nature of how he was built as an image bearer and how the garden itself was built to bring God glory. The cultivation and service would be specific bodily action in the garden that Adam would have rendered as worship unto the King of the universe. The focus of the verse, then, is not anthropocentric or even vaguely biocentric but overtly theocentric. The focus falls primarily on the King . . . not on his garden.

Adam's calling and purpose was very specifically to a life of worship in the garden before God. In the words of the New Testament—in whatever Adam did, he was to do it "to the glory of God" (1 Cor 10:31). The same is then true for all of us. God built us to be worshippers who are to do all things for his glory. As J. I. Packer affirms, "This is what humans are

---

24. Umberto Cassuto, *A Commentary on the Book of Genesis* (Jerusalem: Magnes, 1978), 122.

25. John H. Sailhamer, "Genesis," in *The Expositor's Bible Commentary*, vol. 2, *Genesis, Exodus, Leviticus, Numbers*, ed. Walter C. Kaiser and Bruce K. Waltke (Grand Rapids, MI: Regency, 1990), 45.

made to do, and in one sense we are human only to the extent that we are doing it."[26]

In summary of this point, and in consideration of Gen 2:15, it is right and proper to conclude that in the safety of the flawless environment that God provided, Adam was created and placed in the garden to worship God and demonstrate that worship through obedience. It is the Creator who is the center point of the story, not the creation. "In the beginning God . . ." Certainly this obedience included care and proper management of the earth. Certainly it included serving it, nurturing it, and helping it to flourish. It would be inappropriate to not consider these elements in the discussion. Ultimately, however, from a properly theocentric perspective that recognizes the creation taking place through the agency of the Second Person of the Trinity, any emphasis on "serving the earth" must be placed within the larger *and dominant* category of worshipping God.

John Calvin once wrote that "God cannot bear with seeing his glory appropriated by the creature in even the smallest degree, so intolerable to him is the sacrilegious arrogance of those who, by praising themselves, obscure his glory as far as they can."[27] We would add that not only is it intolerable for people to appropriate God's glory in any way, so also is it inappropriate to allow anything in creation to deflect away from God any glory he is due. It is for this reason we believe that in establishing a theocentric foundation for creation, we must use great precision and careful use of language so as to focus all attention toward the *True North* of glorifying God. Thus, even though it is right to recognize that the created order has a God-given inherent value and that Adam's job included service to the earth, we affirm that ultimately Adam's work was emphatically *not* done for the sake of the earth itself. He cultivated and served as worship rendered to the King of the universe.

It is our conviction, then, that it is in this proper directional ordering toward the *True North* of giving God all glory and praise that Adam (and all humanity) was built and that all he was (and we are) flows out from the glory of God and is to return unto God the glory he is due (*exitus-reditus*). All service rendered in any area of life is meant to be done unto the Lord as a beautiful offering of worship, and it is to be done in accordance with that basic structure of the universe perceivable via the natural and revealed law of God. As John Murray puts it, "The biblical ethic, as it would have been exemplified in a sinless world and as it is

---

26. Packer, *Concise Theology*, 71.

27. John Calvin, *Commentary on Psalm 9*.

exemplified in redeemed humanity, knows no antithesis between duty performed in obedience to commandment and love as the fulfillment of the law."[28] Thus, the primary motivation for creation care boils down to worshipping and obeying in a manner that transcends mere duty-bound service and that will lead to experiencing life's highest joys and God's fullest blessings as each image bearer rightly orders his worship toward *True North*: the glory of God.

Of course, this discussion leads us naturally to the question: how are image bearers to properly "obey" God and properly order their worship unto him—especially in relation to caring for his created order? With this question in mind, we turn to a closer examination of Gen 1:28.

Genesis 1:28—Subdue and Rule: The Image Bearer's Principled Instructions for Worshipful Obedience

> And God blessed them: and God said to them, "Be fruitful and multiply, and fill the earth, and subdue it; and rule over the fish of the sea and over the birds of the sky, and over every living thing that moves on the earth." (Gen 1:28)

A. The Controversy Surrounding Christians and Genesis 1:28. In 1967, medieval historian Lynn White Jr. published a now widely disseminated article that asserted Christianity was to blame for the current and ongoing ecological crisis. The article is fascinating in its claims and is worth quoting key sections at length. White writes,

> What we do about ecology depends on our ideas of the man-nature relationship. More science and more technology are not going to get us out of the present ecologic crisis until we find a new religion, or rethink our old one . . . , the present increasing disruption of the global environment is the product of a dynamic technology and science which were originated in the Western medieval world. . . . Their growth cannot be understood historically apart from distinctive attitudes toward nature which are deeply grounded in Christian dogma. The fact that most people do not think of these attitudes as Christian is irrelevant. No new set of basic values has been accepted in our society to displace those of Christianity. *Hence we shall continue to have a worsening ecologic crisis until we reject the Christian axiom that nature has no reason for*

---

28. John Murray, *Principles of Conduct* (Grand Rapids, MI: Eerdmans, 1957), 37–39.

existence save to serve man. . . . Both our present science and our present
technology are so tinctured with orthodox Christian arrogance toward
nature that no solution for our ecologic crisis can be expected from
them alone. Since the roots of our trouble are so largely religious, the
remedy must also be essentially religious.[29]

Shortly after its publication, White's article seemed to take on a life of
its own. The idea that Christianity was the problem resonated with many
within the environmental movement who were already turning toward
the (at the time) fresh influx of Eastern religions into the United States.
Alister McGrath notes that even though "the intellectual roots of this
attitude turned out to be surprisingly shallow," White's work "became a
sacred text, passed on with an almost uncritical reverence. Many ecologists would no more criticize White's article than fundamentalist Christians would criticize the Bible."[30]

Much of White's critique (and that of those critical of Christianity)
rested on the assumption that the teaching of the Bible in Gen 1:28
instructing Adam and Eve to "subdue" and "rule" over creation was in
essence a license for humankind to exploit the created realm. The argument that "nature has no reason for existence save to serve man" was
founded on the claim that Gen 1:28 gave Adam and Eve unlimited
dominion to do as they pleased for themselves. While certainly there have
been places and times within human history when "Christians" acted
exactly as White claimed, such a reality by no means indicates that the
basic teachings of Christianity actually support such a position.[31] Indeed,
we would suggest that to the degree any blame fall on Christianity, it
should not be on the Christian teachings *per se* but on persons wrongly
acting in the name of Christianity or wrongly interpreted Christian doctrine. An exploration of the Gen 1:28 text will help us demonstrate why
this is so.[32]

B. Two Key Words: "Subdue" and "Rule." Regardless of whether the
claims made against Christianity by White have substance or not, there
can be no doubt that Gen 1:28 gives to humanity a form of *headship* over
the rest of creation. The words "subdue" and "rule" make that clear. Once

---

29. Lynn White Jr., "The Historical Roots of Our Ecological Crisis," *Science* 155, no. 3767 (March 10, 1967), emphasis mine. Accessible on the Internet at http://www.zbi.ee/~kalevi/lwhite.htm.

30. Alister McGrath, *The Reenchantment of Nature: The Denial of Religion and the Ecological Crisis* (New York: Doubleday, 2002), xv–xvi.

31. Bouma-Prediger, *For the Beauty of the Earth*, 74.

32. Francis Schaeffer, *Pollution and the Death of Man* (Wheaton, IL: Crossway, 1970), 59.

again, an in-depth examination of the meaning of these words and their context in Genesis 1 and 2 proves helpful.

First, the word "subdue" in the Hebrew is *kabash*. This word appears in the Old Testament 15 different times in various contexts. Its root meaning relates to treading something down. In its various contexts it can mean:

1. to conquer an enemy (Num 32:22,29; 2 Sam 8:11; Zech 9:15);
2. to bring conquered people under military control (Josh 18:1);
3. to bring people into subjection (1 Chr 22:18; 2 Chr 28:10);
4. to bring into slavery (Neh 5:5; Jer 34:11,16);
5. to tread our sins under foot (Mic 7:19);
6. to molest the queen (Esth 7:8).

As Young points out, the image often depicted in *kabash* "is that of a conqueror putting his foot on the neck of a conquered enemy (see Josh 10:24)."[33] He goes on to point out that "when used of the earth [*kabash*] denotes exercising some form of control or power over nature. The object of *kabash* is the earth, which must be understood as all creation, not simply the physical earth, for the following thought expands it to include living creatures."[34]

The other word in question is "rule," which is a translation of the Hebrew word *radah,* which is also frequently translated (in the KJV for example) as "have dominion." This word appears more than 20 times in the Old Testament, and its root meaning implies the trampling down of something and is often used to show the rule or dominion of a leader over a nation or group of people. In its various contexts it can mean:

1. divine rule over the earth (Pss 72:8; 110:2);
2. Israel ruling over her oppressors (Isa 41:2);
3. nations ruling over Israel (Lev 26:17; Neh 9:28);
4. one nation ruling another (Ezek 29:15);
5. leaders ruling the people (2 Chr 8:10).[35]

This word does not necessarily imply the same strength of rule or submission that *kabash* does. In fact, in several places in the Old Testament, God implores his people not to "rule" (*radah*) harshly or unjustly (Lev 25:43,46; Ezek 34:1–6). Young points out that "when used in reference to creation, [*radah*] would convey the idea of ruling or governing the natural order. The idea conveyed by *radah* is simply to exercise one's right

---

33. Young, *Healing the Earth,* 161–62.
34. Ibid.
35. Ibid., 162.

of rule or authority over another. There is no connotation in the word itself of being harsh or ruthless."[36]

C. Genesis 1:28 in the Context of Theocentric Worship. At this point, in order to determine the proper meaning and usage of these terms in the Gen 1:28 context, we are wise once again to consider the overriding themes we have seen thus far in the creation narratives. First, we recall that in Gen 1:1, God himself is the ultimate subject of the story. This God who is the strong, loving, and careful artisan behind this wondrously created world repeatedly expressed his pleasure with the created realm by indicating that what he saw was "good." We also discovered in this chapter that Gen 1:26–27 depicts God intentionally creating human beings as image bearers who in their very essence are meant to represent God in the created realm. As we explored the meaning of Gen 2:15, we discovered that the created purpose of God's image bearers was to return unto God the glory he as creator alone is due through worshipful obedience.

From this context, then, we can begin to understand that while the words *kabash* ("subdue") and *radah* ("rule") are muscular words of strength and purpose, their objective should not be understood to imply harsh brutality and unlimited tyranny over the earth. Rather, as God's image bearers are instructed to subdue and rule the created order, they are meant to do so as his representatives. Their rule is to be loving, graceful, careful, and purposeful. The strength of their leadership and shaping efforts, then, was meant to be in conformity with the nature of who Adam and Eve were created to be: worshippers who through their joyful obedience would seek to shape the creation in a manner that would increasingly bring glory to their Maker. Ronald Manahan captures the essence of this idea when he writes, "These are certainly forceful terms, but neither by itself necessarily pictures harshness. This element must be supplied by context. These terms are ones of action, *doing* as a consequence of what humans are (image-bearers). The action is formative and shaping, but always as a consequence of what humans are."[37]

One may stop for a moment and wonder why (if the world was without sin or blemish) would the first couple be given the command to "subdue" and "rule" the created order at all. After all, was not the garden already "perfect"? To answer this question, we would simply point out the different possible meanings of the word "perfect." Perfection can be used

36. Ibid.
37. Ronald Manahan, "Christ as the Second Adam," in *The Environment and the Christian*, ed. Calvin B. DeWitt (Grand Rapids, MI: Baker, 1991), 51.

to indicate "without blemish," and it can also be used to indicate "completeness" or "totality." It would seem, then, that in regard to the created order, God did indeed create a world "without blemish" (i.e., perfect, sinless), but that he also created it with room for improvement as Adam and Eve grew in their knowledge and experience of God and his created realm. It seems God made both them and the garden with a capacity for expansion and improvement.

This idea of loving, careful tending motivated by glorious worship is a rich concept with serious and lasting implications for us to consider. If God's image bearers could be restored to such a calling and vision, the implications for creation care would be enormous. This is why we began the chapter with a long quote by Gimli the Dwarf from J. R. R. Tolkien's classic *The Lord of the Rings*. Through this character's awe-filled and respectful joy over the wonders of the Glittering Caves at Helm's Deep, Tolkien captures much of the attitude and motivation that should drive image bearers given the freedom to co-create with God in this wondrous world. With cautious skill, tap by tap, humans working to open up the vast wonders of the created world might gradually yet stunningly enhance the beauty that is there and adorn it with still more beauty that they create.

With this idea in mind, then, we can now identify why the critique of Christianity offered by Lynn White is so off base. The biblical text clearly does not give humans some type of unlimited dominion in which they have absolute rights to do with creation whatever they please. Rather, as unstained image bearers, their worshipful work would always be aligned to *True North*. Working in light of the Gen 1:28 instructions to subdue and rule, they would have been in complete congruence with the eternal law by which God created both them and the universe. Thus, to interpret Gen 1:28 as some type of "cultural mandate" or "dominion mandate" in which fallen sinners can do whatever they please would be a complete misunderstanding of the text and context. Subduing and ruling are simply not mandates "for oppression or sanctions for despotic, totalitarian rule over nature. Approval for the exercise of absolute or unlimited power is alien to Genesis 1 and to the Old Testament as a whole."[38]

Instead, given the context of sinless worshippers asked to subdue and rule, we should understand that God did indeed give them freedom, but the freedom to act was a freedom aligned in complete harmony with God's divine intent, heart, and will. Their relationship with the rest of the

---

38. James A. Nash, *Loving Nature: Ecological Integrity and Christian Responsibility* (Nashville: Abingdon, 1991), 104.

creation order would not have been understood as "an alien duty stemming from a hard command, that is, as a joyless obligation." Rather, they would have acted in respect that involved both wonder and delight.[39] As Vern Poythress puts it, "The 'dominion' of Gen 1:28 is thus to be understood as a thoughtful, caring dominion, a dominion expressing God's goodness and care, and not a heartless, brutal, crushing dominion. Genesis 1–2 repudiates the sinful perversion of dominion into destructive exploitation."[40] In the history of the church, "dominion was taken for granted, but it was usually the dominion of benevolence, not exploitation, and it was assumed that this benevolence was the normative state of Eden."[41]

This is why even Richard Young, whose overall work we greatly appreciate, is wrong on this point when he properly argues against Gen 1:28 being used as an unlimited dominion and cultural mandate but then suggests that it is best understood as an "ecological mandate" and that "God's concern when He finished creation was not our impacting society with theistic values, but taking care of what He had just finished making. This was *preeminent on God's mind*."[42] We beg to differ. Genesis 1:28 is not—emphatically not—an ecological mandate. It is a *worship mandate*! The preeminent thing on God's mind was that all of creation—both human and nonhuman—would reach the heights of their existence by worshipping him and therein finding joys unimaginable. Would that mean they would rightly care for his planet? Certainly. Was caring for the planet his ultimate concern? Certainly not. The primary calling and task of the human being is not care for the garden but worshipping the Creator of the garden.

In light of these truths, then, we come to the conclusion that is diametrically opposed to the accusations made by Lynn White Jr. The solution to our environmental crisis is not in dismissing Christianity and the dominion mandate but in rightly understanding Gen 1:28 as a worship mandate and fully owning it as the most promising way forward!

In the final analysis, the subduing and ruling of Gen 1:28 is clearly meant to indicate that in the fullness of their nature as image bearers, Adam and Eve (and their descendants) where given a mandate to work hard with great joy at the prospect of rendering unto God a continuous,

---

39. H. Paul Santmire, *Brother Earth: Nature, God and Ecology in Time of Crisis* (Nashville: Thomas Nelson, 1970), 86.

40. Vern S. Poythress, *Redeeming Science* (Wheaton, IL: Crossway Books, Good News Publishers, 2006), 150.

41. Nash, *Loving Nature*, 103.

42. Young, *Healing the Earth*, 160–61; emphasis mine.

eternal act of worship in the way they loved, cared for, served, shaped, and stewarded the created realm. That is what they were created for, that is what the garden was created for, and that is how they and it would have fulfilled their ultimate purpose and destiny by aligning with *True North*.

IV. Applying Genesis 1:28—The Principle of Embedded Headship

In order to understanding *how* the human person ought to function as an image bearer created to worship and obey through subduing and ruling, we believe it is important to understand how two more concepts function together and guide human stewardship over the visible creation. The first of these is the biblical notion of headship and submission; the second is the concept of human embeddedness in the creation order.

A. Headship and Submission

Perhaps one of the main reasons people like Lynn White Jr. have made such degrading claims about the nature of Christianity is that they have misunderstood (and Christians have poorly modeled) the principle of headship and submission. Certainly, when poorly understood and modeled, headship and submission can take on the flavor of tyranny and oppression. Sadly, many human governments and marriages have used Christian language to justify horrific acts of injustice and sinful oppression. As we will develop in the next chapter, due to the pervasive nature of human sin, this should not surprise us.

On the other hand, however, throughout Scripture when headship and submission are properly understood and appropriately applied, a beautiful picture emerges. Consider, for example, the picture of biblical headship and submission between a husband and wife as taught by the apostle Paul in the fifth chapter of the book of Ephesians. Paul instructs wives to submit to their husbands as unto the Lord, then immediately instructs husbands to set the context for such submission by loving their wives "as Christ also loved the church and gave himself up for her, so that He might sanctify her, having cleansed her by the washing of water with the word" (Eph 5:25–26). He then goes on, crucially, to indicate that the loving service and sacrifice so often a part of headship is initiated and done so that like Christ, whose headship over the church brings it to a higher place of beauty before the throne of God ("that He might present to Himself the church in all her glory," v. 27), a husband's headship seeks to increase the beauty of his bride in the eyes of God (Eph 5:22–33). The emphasis is clearly not on the husband having someone serve him. Rather, as head giving the kind of care that Christ gives the church would require loving, careful, studious, sacrificial, yet joyful work.

Likewise with the created order, as we pointed out above, the headship humans are given over creation is not to be harsh, oppressive tyranny. Human beings, as image bearers, stand under the authority of God and only rightly act in headship as they rightly represent him and his wishes. James Nash helps shed light on this idea when he explains that Adam and Eve were to interact with the created order like royal ambassadors. Understood in the context of the ancient Near East (in which the Genesis narratives were penned), such an ambassador was given dominion to act as a "viceroy" in the ruler's stead. This delegated authority was to be neither oppressive nor unlimited in its expression. The position was given with the understanding that usurping the king's authority or ethical standards was wrong.[43] Thus, the principle of headship in the name of the triune God connotes just and benevolent governance as well as sacrificial leadership, all rendered back to the King for his joy and glory.

B. Embeddedness

In his book *A Moral Climate*, Michael Northcott asserts that "at the heart of the pathology of ecological crisis is the refusal of modern humans to see themselves as creatures, contingently embedded in networks of relationships with other creatures, and with the Creator."[44] While we would be hesitant to give the same ultimate emphasis to this point, we believe Northcott's comments helpfully point toward a key element of "subduing" and "ruling" as worship: humans must remember that, like the rest of creation, they are created beings and are a part of creation. They do not stand over and against it. Like the rest of creation, human beings are created, finite, contingent beings. As such, they are a part of the created realm and are embedded in it. We can understand this "embeddedness" in two ways.

First, Gen 2:7 indicates that human beings have a *dualistic* nature comprised of both a material or physical element and an immaterial or spiritual/soulish element.

---

43. Nash, *Loving Nature*, 104.
44. Michael. S. Northcott, *A Moral Climate: The Ethics of Global Warming* (London: Darton, Longman and Todd, 2007), 16.

> Then the LORD God formed man of the dust from the ground, and
> breathed into his nostrils the breath of life; and man became a living
> being.

From this text we see that not only are we bodies, but we are bodies that
are made alive by the "breath of life" that God gives to all living creatures.
What sets humans apart from all living creatures is not the fact that we
have the breath of life, but that in receiving the breath of life we also
are made image bearers. The immaterial part of human life that is different from all other animals that breathe is what we learned from Gen
1:26–28: humans alone bear the image of God. As it relates to our discussion here, what Gen 2:7 helps us to understand is the fact that when
God breathed life "into" the body, he made us what Gilbert Meilaender
describes as "embodied selves."[45] That is, the immaterial and the material
elements are integrally and necessarily linked.

The fact that there is an integration of the body and soul is what marks
the Christian perspective as vastly distinct from Platonic thought as
well as that of Buddhist and Hindu teachings. In Greek anthropological
understanding, Plato likened the soul to a bird and the body to a cage. As
he understood it, not only was the soul the more important element, but
it existed independently of the body. Thus, as a bird is trapped in a cage,
so also is the human soul trapped in the body. His anthropology was
a full-blown *dualism*. The teachings of the Eastern religions are similar
in regard to the perspective on the material body. The physical realm is
either understood as an illusion or as fundamentally corrupt and thus in
need of denial if one is to reach enlightenment or Nirvana. It should be
obvious, then, that because the soul is more valuable, these perspectives
consequently render the status of the body to a significantly lower level
of value than the soul.

Christian theology, however, takes a much different view about nature
and the body. It understands that while there is a *duality* that exists with
body and soul, there is no full-blown *dualism* taught by the Scriptures.[46]
To clarify the distinction we are making between duality and dualism,
we would argue that while each of us has both a body and soul (duality), these elements are not meant to function independently (dualism).
Rather, as Gen 2:7 describes it, God breathes life *into* the body. There

---

45. Gilbert Meilaender, "Respect for Persons and their Agency," in *On Moral Medicine: Theological Perspectives in Medical Ethics*, ed. Stephen E. Lammers and Allen Verhey (Grand Rapids, MI:
Eerdmans, 1998), 395.

46. See Charles Ryrie's discussion of this point in *Basic Theology* (Wheaton, IL: Victor, 1986),
195.

is an integration of body and soul, material and immaterial. It is this integration of the body and soul that God describes in the Genesis text as "very good."[47] Clearly the implication from this point is that not only are spiritual matters important to God, so also are bodily matters. God is pleased to give us both body and soul. J. I. Packer explains,

> The embodiment of the soul is integral to God's design for mankind. Through the body . . . we are to experience our environment, enjoy and control things around us, and relate to other people. There was nothing evil or corruptible about the body as God first made it, and had sin not come in, the physical ailing, aging, and rotting that leads to death as we know it would have been no part of human life."[48]

Humans are not only embedded in creation, our immaterial/soulish selves are integrated into a unified whole with our physical body. The Genesis 1 creation account also clearly indicates that human beings are created very specifically as a part of the creation order to be participants in it. As Gen 1:24–28 indicates, the creation of man was not given a separate day from the animals, but rather they were created among the animals on the sixth day.

For both of these reasons, then, we affirm not only that our bodies and our world are gifts from God, but even more so we recognize that in God declaring them to be "good" and part of a created order that is "very good," Christianity is a nature-affirming faith system vastly superior to Greek philosophies and Buddhist and Hindu spiritualities with regard to its perspective on the created order. Within Christianity it is appropriate and right not only to affirm the material world but also to enjoy it and revel in it as a gift from the Lord.

Embedded Headship

In order to see how these two principles (headship and embeddedness) integrate in this ethics of worship, we begin by recognizing that while humans are created on the same day as the rest of the animals, the Genesis 1 account of creation very specifically makes a distinction between animals who are created "after their kind" and humans who are made in

---

47. While the particular reference for "very good" in Gen 1:31 refers to the totality of the created realm, the point is that the material and spiritual are both affirmed. For a fuller discussion of this, see J. P. Moreland and Scott B. Rae, *Body and Soul: Human Nature and the Crisis in Ethics* (Downers Grove, IL: InterVarsity, 2000).

48. Packer, *Concise Theology*, 75.

the image of God. In addition, it is only the creation of human beings on the sixth day that receives special description in Gen 2:4–25. Thus, while there is a fundamental link between humans and the rest of creation in regard to the manner in which they were created, there is also recognition of important differences that place humans in the unique place of dual representatives. On the one hand, they are to represent God to the rest of the visible created order as image bearers, and on the other hand, they are to represent the visible created order before God through the God-given position of headship.

In his *Pollution and the Death of Man*, Francis Schaeffer illustrates this dual role humans have by using a chart that we have adapted in order to aid in understanding this point.[49]

God as an Infinite Being	God as a Personal Being
Chasm or Gap	Humans
Humans	*Chasm or Gap*
Animal	Animal
Plant	Plant
Machine	Machine

Because God is both personal and yet infinite in nature, the human being will relate to him in distinct ways represented in the chart by the two columns. In the left-hand column, which illustrates man's relationship to God in his infinity (noncommunicable attributes), there is a great chasm that exists ontologically between God and human beings. As Schaeffer explains it, the infinite God "creates all things . . . [but] only He is infinite, and only He is the Creator; everything else is dependent. So man, the animal, the flower, and the machine, in the biblical viewpoint, are equally separated from God in that he created them all. On the side of infinity, man is as separated from God as is the machine."[50]

In this sense, humans are not like God, yet they have an affinity with all the rest of creation. In humility and dependence, then, the image bearer looks downward and recognizes that he is a part of the created

---

49. Adapted from Francis Schaeffer, *Pollution and the Death of Man* (Wheaton, IL: Crossway, 1970), 48. Used by permission of Crossway, a publishing ministry of Good News Publishers, Wheaton, IL 60187, <http://www.crossway.org>. We have slightly modified the chart in order to make it simpler (we hope) for the reader to understand.

50. Ibid., 48–49.

order and is embedded within it (Gen 1:1–25). As one embedded in the created order, the image bearer is wise to recognize that to hurt this created realm hurts himself. While this is true, he also recognizes that as an image bearer, he has the "highest" place among the created order, and so he is responsible to act "upward" in presenting himself and the rest of creation to God.[51]

On the other hand, in the right-hand column, we see that in relation to God as a personal being, "the animal, the flower, and the machine are below the chasm. On the side of God's infinity everything else is equally separated from God; but on the side of His personality, God has created man in His own image."[52] Here the image-bearing status separates humans from the rest of creation and allows us to uniquely relate to God both rationally and morally. Our source of meaning comes from above, and our unique role in the created order is as representatives of God downward toward the "lower" elements of creation in which we are embedded.

In this sense, the human has a special affinity with God and thus represents God to the created order in a special way. He first of all finds his meaning from looking upward to God (Gen 2:15). Then he is to provide headship to the created order by subduing it and ruling over it and presenting it before the Lord as an act of personal worship and as part of an entire chorus of worship sung by the entire created realm (Gen 1:26–28).

As Schaeffer puts it, man has "two relationships—upward and downward." He finds his ultimate meaning and purpose by focusing upward toward God, yet he lives out his life and expresses his full humanity in the context of the created realm of which he is a part. Thus, as he relates to the rest of creation, he is able to recognize that he is separate from it in one sense, yet related to it in another.[53]

---

51. Millard Erickson adds some further distinction to how the beings in the created realm relate to God. He writes, "The Physical Creation obeys Him *mechanically.* It functions according to natural laws with which it has been structured. The animals obey God *instinctively.* Their actions manifest impulses God divinely implanted within them. Humans, however, have the capacity to obey God *voluntarily.* They can choose to obey or disobey." See "Biblical Theology of Ecology" in *The Earth Is the Lord's: Christians and the Environment*, ed. Richard D. Land and Louis A. Moore (Nashville: Broadman, 1992), 39.

52. Schaeffer, *Pollution*, 48–49.

53. For a further discussion on this topic, we recommend Manahan's article "Christ as the Second Adam," 45–56. Manahan does a nice job arguing that humans actually stand in a threefold relationship with God, others, and the created world. We see the value in this argument but, for reasons of simplicity, have adopted Schaeffer's model more directly and subsumed the horizontal relationship with other humans into the discussion of Adam and Eve's responsibilities toward the created order. Nonetheless, as the following paragraphs unfold, our obvious concern for the horizontal human-to-human aspects of creation care will become obvious.

Based on this, Schaeffer argues that "we should treat each thing with integrity because it is the way God has made it. . . . The value of the things is not in themselves autonomously, but that God made them— and thus they deserve to be treated with high respect. The tree in the field is to be treated with high respect." This respect, however, is not unlimited and does not rise to the level of respect one would show a person. As Schaeffer puts it, "it is not to be romanticized . . . when you drive the axe into the tree when you need firewood, you are not cutting down a person; you are cutting down a tree."[54]

On the other hand, fellow human beings, though they are part of the creation order and must be treated with respect, are also persons like God. Their value as persons, then, is inherently higher because among all the created animals only humans bear the image of God. Thus we see another limit to the form of dominion he is allowed. God prohibits the wrongful taking of human life and describes it as "murder" (Exod 20:13). Unequivocally, then, if one is properly committed to creation care as an act of worship before the King of the universe, then he or she must understand and be ardently committed to protecting the sacredness of human life. The wrongful death of fellow image bearers—unborn children, for example—is completely contrary to creation-care advocacy. Anyone who is "pro-creation-care" should by definition be "pro-life."

In sum, we believe Vern Poythress captures the heart of this principle of *embedded headship* when he writes,

> Genesis 1–2. On the one hand, it does not simply immerse man in nature so that he is just one more species, with no special privileges. Man is special. And his specialness does not consist first of all in his superior intelligence but in his status as a creature made in the image of God. Hence, we do not worship nature or place animals on the same level as man. Unlike some people who want to leave nature completely untouched, we can confidently domesticate animals or plant a garden that alters the untouched wilderness.
>
> On the other hand, Genesis repudiates the view that man has carte blanche to do whatever suits him and to satisfy his own lusts at any price. God cares for his creation; he does not exploit it. Man must imitate God. Certainly man may use the fruit of the trees for his nourishment (Gen 2:16), but his overall goal is to serve and glorify God, not merely serve his own desires.[55]

---

54. Schaeffer, *Pollution*, 54.
55. Poythress, *Redeeming Science*, 150.

In concluding this point, we would reaffirm Michael Northcott's point in saying that it is problematic when (for whatever reason) humans refuse to see themselves properly as contingent created beings who are embedded in relationships with other creatures and with God.[56] Likewise, it is also a problem when humans refuse to recognize (or they improperly enact) their responsibility to represent God to the created order as image bearers. We get into trouble when in arrogance we either usurp the position of authority and exploit the earth through harsh dominion or we forget that we are a part of the created order and act as if our impact on it does not affect our own lives or the nature of the entire created realm's worship of God.

V. Conclusion: "Very Good"

Genesis 1:31

> God saw all that He had made, and behold, it was very good. And there was evening and there was morning, the sixth day.

In this and the previous chapter, we have engaged in an analysis of the Genesis creation accounts with an eye for understanding how the doctrine of God should shape our understanding of the doctrine of creation and then in turn shape our foundational perspective on the ethics of creation care. The focus of this chapter in particular has been on the unique position human beings enjoy in the created realm. Not only are they created in the image of God, but they have been given a very specific calling and directional purpose to worship and obey the King of the universe and render unto him all glory that he is due. In this light, God instructed Adam and Eve to "subdue" the earth and "rule" over it so that not only their own lives but all of creation would forever be aligned with *True North*: bringing all praise and glory to God.

By way of conclusion, only a few ideas remain to be explored before we turn our attention more particularly to the role of Jesus Christ as the Redeemer—who through his life, death, and resurrection brings the possibility of healing and restoration to the entire created realm.

---

56. Northcott, *A Moral Climate*, 16. Anthony Weston makes the same basic point in his introduction in *An Invitation to Environmental Philosophy*, ed. Anthony Weston (Oxford: Oxford University Press, 1999), 2.

First, as we learn from Gen 1:31, God looked back over all the work he accomplished in his six days of creating and gave a final evaluation of "very good." Prior to this pronouncement, he had declared the created order "good" six times and thus gave strong affirmation to the worth and value of the nonhuman created order. Now, however, after completing his creation of man and woman, God sums up the entire process with the superlative pronouncement. He is very pleased with what he has made! "Like a master chef bringing a multicourse banquet before admiring guests, God kisses his fingers with each new delicacy that he brings from his creative workshop, until, after the *piece de resistance*, in a seventh and final verdict on the whole achievement, God declare it all 'very good.' The whole wonderful meal has been a triumph of the chef's skill and art."[57]

Certainly, then, we understand that the addition of Adam and Eve, the only creatures in the creation accounts identified as image bearers, holds a special place in God's created realm. Indeed, "the degree of glory increases with the elevation in the scale, so that the human being brings greater glory to the Maker by honoring Him than do the rock or the plant."[58] Yet, one should not make the mistake in asserting that the pronouncement of "very good" is related specifically to human beings apart from the rest of the created order. No, for while it is only after the humans are introduced that he saw that it was very good, in context "the statement refers to God seeing all that He had made. Thus, it appears that the completeness of the creation is what stimulated God's extra pleasure."[59]

Paul Santmire's comments capture the idea,

> In Genesis 1:31, immediately following the completion of God's creative activity with the creation of man, the words "*very good*" are used for the first time. It might be assumed that these words imply that God bestows superior approval on the creature for whose sake he began to create the world. But such an interpretation would be too narrow. The "very good" of Genesis 1:31 refers to the whole . . . the text does not suggest that God sees man *alone* as very good. Of course the creation would not be "very good," . . . without man. But—and this is the point—neither would it be "very good" without the whole of nature.

---

57. Wright, *The Mission of God*, 398. Wright credits Huw Spanner for the idea of this metaphor, "Tyrants, Stewards—or Just Kings?" in *Animals on the Agenda: Questions About Animals for Theology and Ethics*, ed. Andrew Linzey and Dorothy Yamamoto (London: SCM, 1998), 218.

58. Erickson, "Biblical Theology of Ecology," in Land and Moore, *The Earth Is the Lord's*, 39.

59. Ibid., 44.

> When God looks at all the results of his creative activity, he takes joy
> in every thing he sees.[60]

Thus we can now say in conclusion, as well as in a recapitulation of
the main theme of our study, that from the very beginning of Christ's
work in creation, the focal point of the story is not only about him and
the work that he does but also about his evaluation of the entire event
and purpose of creation. The fact that the whole created realm is "very
good" is not simply a factor of its existence. No, it is "very good" because
it existed exactly as God wanted it to and because in that alignment with
God's eternal law and plan, all of the creation was built to work together
as a unified whole that would resound with the praises and glory of God.

From the beginning, God's intention was that the whole of creation,
not just human beings, but certainly led by them, would sing His praise
in worship, and this unified chorus would bring God pleasure (Pss 89:5;
96:9; Isa 43:20a; 66:23). This is *True North*. Right attitudes about creation care, therefore, are directly linked to genuinely spiritual and truth-
ful worship of the Lord of creation, Jesus Christ (John 4:23–24).

---

60. Santmire, *Brother Earth*, 83.

4

Christ the Incarnate and Resurrected Redeemer

The Lord Jesus Christ took off His royal robes in heaven, came to earth to be born of a virgin, lived a sinless life, and died upon a cross—pouring out His rich, red, royal blood as an atonement for your sin and to satisfy the righteous demands of a holy God.[1]

Biblical hope, rooted in the incarnation and resurrection, is creational, this-worldly, visible, physical, bodily hope.[2]

I. Introduction

I n the tenth chapter of the book of Jeremiah, the prophet declares that God is the one "Who made the earth by His power, Who established the world by His wisdom" and who by his understanding has "stretched out the heavens" (Jer 10:12). God, he declares, is "the Maker of all" (Jer 10:16). It is no surprise, then, that because he is the Maker of all things, both the inanimate and the animated elements of creation are designed to "declare the glory of God" (Ps 19:17 NIV).

In the previous chapter we explored the purpose and function for which God created human beings as a part of his created order. Of particular note we explored at some length the important connection between Gen 2:15 and Gen 1:28. In this process we discovered that human beings—unique among all the created realm as image bearers—were placed in the

---

1. Adrian Rodgers and Tom Fox, *The Wonder of It All* (Nashville: B&H, 2001), 54.
2. Herman Bavinck, *Reformed Dogmatics: Holy Spirit, Church, and New Creation*, vol. 4, ed. John Bolt, trans. John Vriend (Grand Rapids, MI: Baker, 2008), 715.

garden to worship God and obey him through their service, protection, and cultivation of the garden. With this disposition of worshipful obedience, human beings were also designed and positioned by God to lovingly and carefully fill out their calling of "embedded headship" toward and over the rest of nature.

In this context, then, Millard Erickson rightly points out that

> God's creation was for definite purposes. Man was intended to know, love, and obey God. He was to live in harmony with his fellow man. . . . And he was certainly placed here upon earth to exercise dominion over the rest of creation. But these relationships and this function presuppose something else. Man is most fully man when he is active in these relationships and performs this function, for he is then fulfilling his telos, God's purpose for him.[3]

In sum, we discovered in the previous couple of chapters that God made human beings his special agents to provide a loving headship over the entire visible creation. Their job was to nurture, grow, direct, and lead it toward its ultimate end—*True North*. And what Erickson reminds us is that only when human beings live and lead in this context and for this end will they both fulfill the inherent purpose for which they were created and experience the fullness of their humanity as well as God's joy.

Unfortunately, as the ever-present environmental degradations that surround us potently remind us, things are not the way they were created and designed to be. What we learn from Scripture is that it is that Adam and Eve, through their sin and rebellion, brought corruption upon not only themselves but also all of humanity and the entire created realm.

It is the purpose of this chapter to explore the nature and implications of this "fall" and then to examine the redemptive work of Jesus Christ to once again rightly align both human beings and the entire created realm to the original purpose for which he created it.

II. The Fall

As we noted in our introductory chapter, much of the discussion and debate about creation care and environmental ethics revolves around what appears to many to be tremendous and increasing levels of crisis due to a number of manmade environmental degradations. Putting aside

---

3. Millard Erickson, *Christian Theology* (Grand Rapids, MI: Baker, 1983), 513–14.

for a moment the particulars of the debates about what the causes are, and the extent of these degradations, there is no doubt that humans pollute the air, contaminate water systems, endanger animal species, and even tragically destroy the life of other human beings through murder, wars of aggression, abortion, and any number of injustices. In light of the wondrous glories set before Adam and Eve in Genesis 1 and 2, one can only wonder, "How did we get here?"

Genesis 3

Following the creation narratives of Genesis 1 and 2, we find the account of the first human sin in Genesis 3 and there discover the tragic reason why humans, and the entire visible created realm, are no longer rightly aligned to *True North*.

> Now the serpent was more crafty than any beast of the field which the
> LORD God had made. And he said to the woman, "Indeed, has God
> said, 'You shall not eat from any tree of the garden'?" The woman said
> to the serpent, "From the fruit of the trees of the garden we may eat;
> but from the fruit of the tree which is in the middle of the garden, God
> has said, 'You shall not eat from it or touch it, or you will die.'" The
> serpent said to the woman, "You surely will not die! "For God knows
> that in the day you eat from it your eyes will be opened, and you will
> be like God, knowing good and evil." When the woman saw that the
> tree was good for food, and that it was a delight to the eyes, and that
> the tree was desirable to make *one* wise, she took from its fruit and ate;
> and she gave also to her husband with her, and he ate. Then the eyes
> of both of them were opened, and they knew that they were naked;
> and they sewed fig leaves together and made themselves loin coverings.
> (Gen 3:1–7)

One cannot help but notice when reading this text of Scripture the incredible deception that must have taken place. Here are Adam and Eve together in the fullness of God's bounty, where they are given freedom to eat from any tree save one. Lest we miss the point, they not only had access to the full *bounty* of God, they also had uninhibited access to God *himself*! As the text will go on to imply (Gen 3:8–13), they had the unimaginable freedom to walk with God and talk with God and enjoy his very presence. Yet, somehow they find themselves contemplating and discussing with Satan the only thing expressly forbidden to them by the very One who created them, loved them, and set them free to flourish in the abundance of divine grace.

Thus it was that in the presence of untold wonders, in rejection of the inherent purpose and orientation of their being, and in outright defiance of God himself, Adam and Eve exchanged the infinite riches of the glory of God for a piece of fruit. In so doing, our first parents squandered paradise and plunged all of creation into the fall.

It is important to understand that "Adam and Eve's fall into sin was not just an isolated act of disobedience but an event of catastrophic significance for creation as a whole. The effects of sin touch all of creation; no created thing is in principle untouched by the corrosive effects of the fall. . . ."[4] We see the evidence of this in the next couple of verses in the biblical account.

> They heard the sound of the LORD God walking in the garden in the cool of the day, and the man and his wife hid themselves from the presence of the LORD God among the trees of the garden. Then the LORD God called to the man, and said to him, "Where are you?" He said, "I heard the sound of You in the garden, and I was afraid because I was naked; so I hid myself." And He said, "Who told you that you were naked? Have you eaten from the tree of which I commanded you not to eat?" The man said, "The woman whom You gave *to be* with me, she gave me from the tree, and I ate." Then the LORD God said to the woman, "What is this you have done?" And the woman said, "The serpent deceived me, and I ate." (Gen 3:8–13)

Perhaps the most tragic verses in the Bible, we see in these lines the unimaginable cost of rebellion. Apparently familiar with the very sounds of God's footsteps, they now cower and hide from the One they used to stand before in full assurance and blessing. The once intimate and joyful sound of his approach now becomes the basis for fear and doubt. In a scene that would be laughable if not for its sheer awfulness, these two image bearers actually try to hide themselves from the sovereign, omniscient, omnipotent God of the universe. Once "discovered," the best they can do by way of explanation is to blame-shift and seek to justify themselves. It seems the pattern of human response to sin was indelibly put in place that day.

---

4. Albert M. Wolters, *Creation Regained: Biblical Basics for a Reformational Worldview*, 2nd ed. (Grand Rapids, MI: Eerdmans, 2005), 53.

With this contextual background in place, then, we see two very significant points emerge that relate directly to our larger discussion of environmental ethics:

> Then to Adam He said, "Because you have listened to the voice of your wife, and have eaten from the tree about which I commanded you, saying, 'You shall not eat from it'; Cursed is the ground because of you; / In toil you will eat of it / All the days of your life. / Both thorns and thistles it shall grow for you; / And you will eat the plants of the field; / By the sweat of your face / You will eat bread, / Till you return to the ground, / Because from it you were taken; / For you are dust, / And to dust you shall return." (Gen 3:17–19)

First, note that the text indicates that an immediate consequence of the fall was that the nonhuman elements of the created order were affected. The ground, which God declared to be "good" in Gen 1:9–10, became "cursed" because of Adam's sin. Only through laborious hardship would it now yield its fruits. Note that the text does not say that the ground sinned, but rather, as a consequence of human rebellion, the created order itself was now affected. It appears, from this, that in some way the entire material created order was bound up with Adam's moral standing before the Creator and Lord.

Second, the promised result of death from sin (Gen 2:17) now also began to take effect in Adam's body. In v. 17 we see that God (who had used that good ground he created to form Adam and integrate into him the breath of life and the image of God) now informs Adam that he will die and his body will return to the ground. From that point on, Adam (and all of his race) would experience in his own body a slow degradation, until finally, someday, physical death would take him (Gen 5:5).

Not only did physical death result from sin, on the day that Adam and Eve ate the fruit; they were banished from the loving presence of God—a spiritual death that is fundamentally related to their disordering from God and his purposes. This death, the Scriptures will later confirm, is an exclusion from the loving presence of God for eternity future, unless the relationship is restored by some other means (see, e.g., Eph 2:1–10). On this point, Tom Schreiner comments:

> The account in Genesis 3 reveals that Adam died when he sinned, for upon sinning he was immediately separated from God. Adam's hiding from God and his expulsion from the garden signals his spiritual separation from God. I am not suggesting that physical death and spiritual

death can ultimately be separated, for the former is the culmination and outworking of the latter. Nonetheless, the account in Genesis indicates that death is fundamentally separation from God, and this alienation from God entered the world through Adam's sin.[5]

Therefore, the biblical meaning of death in this context "includes physical death, but is not restricted to this. The immediate context prompts us to look deeper, and we see that there is a spiritual death also associated with banishment from God's loving presence and withdrawal of his blessing."[6]

Albert Wolters expands on the enormity of this point when he writes, "Wherever anything wrong exists in the world, anything we experience as anti-normative, evil, distorted, or sick, there we meet the perversion of God's good creation. It is one of the unique and distinct features of the Bible's teaching on the human situation that all evil and perversity in the world is ultimately the result of humanity's fall, of its refusal to live according to the good ordinances of God's creation."[7]

Now corrupted by sin and separated from a loving and whole relationship with God, Adam and Eve are commanded to leave the safety of Eden and are cast out of the garden.

> Therefore the LORD God sent him out from the garden of Eden, to cultivate the ground from which he was taken. So He drove the man out; and at the east of the garden of Eden He stationed the cherubim and the flaming sword which turned every direction to guard the way to the tree of life. (Gen 3:23–24)

No longer in the "temple of worship" that God created the garden to be, and no longer rightly ordered to his Creator or his created purpose, Adam is sent out from the garden to "cultivate" the ground. We are reminded from our discussion in the previous chapter that Gen 2:15 indicates that as image bearers, humans were built to worship and obey. Here we see the first signs that while his fundamental structuring as a worshipper does not change, the content and direction of his worship does. J. I. Packer writes that the fall "diminished God's image not only in Adam and Eve

---

5. Thomas R. Schreiner, *Romans*, Baker Exegetical Commentary on the New Testament, ed. Moises Silva (Grand Rapids, MI: Baker, 1998), 272.

6. Steve Jeffery, Michael Ovey, and Andrew Sach, *Pierced for Our Transgressions* (Wheaton, IL: Crossway, 2007), 121. For more discussion on this point, see also Douglas J. Moo's commentary on Romans in *The NIV Application Commentary: Romans* (Grand Rapids, MI: Zondervan, 2000), 181.

7. Wolters, *Creation Regained*, 55.

but in all their descendants, that is, the whole human race. We retain the image structurally, in the sense that our humanity is intact, but not functionally, for we are now sin's slaves and unable to use our powers to mirror God's holiness."[8]

Thus, as Adam and Eve were sent out of the garden, their worship would continue, because that is what they were made to be—worshippers. However, their ordering to *True North* was now lost. Adam and Eve's sin plunged the entire human race into a fundamental disordering of their worship. Once again recalling the Genesis 1 creation narrative, we discovered in verse 28 that God gave a "worship mandate" to Adam and Eve to fill the earth and subdue it and rule over it in such a way that it would bring glory to his name as they expressed their creative abilities as image bearers. Now, however, instead of being sent out of the garden as loving stewards and worshipful shepherds of the created realm, they left distorted and bent, in dishonor and shame. Most importantly, their worship was now misdirected, resulting in both physical and spiritual death.

The Effects of the Fall on Humans and Creation

In relation to consequences that come from the fall, certainly Scripture is replete with indications of how it affects human beings. Paul's letter to the Romans provides a clear and concise explanation. First, we see that Rom 1:18–32 gives certain indication that fundamentally, human worship becomes disordered as a fruit of a rebellious heart. Professing to be wise, image bearers in rebellion actually become fools because we exchange the glory of the incorruptible God for other objects or moral choices that are contrary to *True North*. As Colin Gunton puts it, "The doctrine of original sin holds that somewhere in the past of the human race . . . there took place a determination of the human race to a disrupted or disorderly relation to the God from whom it takes its being."[9]

Second, Rom 5:12 indicates that just as through one man sin entered into the world, and death through sin, so death spread to all men because all sinned. Paul then goes on to indicate in Rom 5:18 that through one transgression there resulted condemnation to all men because through Adam all human beings in his lineage would inherit a sin nature. In other words, "God counted Adam's guilt as belonging to us, and since God is

---

8. J. I. Packer, *Concise Theology: A Guide to Historic Christian Beliefs* (Wheaton, IL: Tyndale, 1993), 72–73.

9. Colin E. Gunton, *Christ and Creation* (Grand Rapids, MI: Eerdmans, 1997), 45.

the ultimate judge of all things in the universe, and since his thoughts are always true, Adam's guilt does in fact belong to us."[10]

Not only have we inherited a sin nature, Rom 3:23 indicates that "all" of us have sinned in our own right and thus have "fall[en] short of the glory of God." Romans 6:23 further indicates that the consequences for our sin nature and personal choices of sin is "death." Thus, like Adam, all of us have inherited a body that will degrade unto physical death, but also like Adam, all of us through sin have been separated from a right relationship with God and are thus destined to an eternity apart from his favor and loving presence unless a right relationship is restored by some other means.

In addition to the effects sin and the fall have on people, Scripture is also clear that human sin takes a toll on the rest of the created order as well. We have already seen that Gen 3:17 indicates that the ground experiences a curse because of Adam's sin. It is in Rom 8:18–23 that we see a fuller discussion of the effect of sin on the rest of creation.

> For I consider that the sufferings of this present time are not worthy to be compared with the glory that is to be revealed to us. For the anxious longing of the creation waits eagerly for the revealing of the sons of God. For the creation was subjected to futility, not willingly, but because of Him who subjected it, in hope that the creation itself also will be set free from its slavery to corruption into the freedom of the glory of the children of God. For we know that the whole creation groans and suffers the pains of childbirth together until now. And not only this, but also we ourselves, having the first fruits of the Spirit, even we ourselves groan within ourselves, waiting eagerly for our adoption as sons, the redemption of our body.

This passage clearly indicates that "the predicament of the whole of creation is tied to the fate of humankind. In Rom 8:20 the apostle Paul speaks of the creation as having been 'subjected to frustration, not by its own choice, but by the will of the one who subjected it.' This is an unmistakable allusion to Gen 3:17, where God cursed the ground in response to Adam's sin, and the whole created order suffers as a result of human rebellion."[11] Thus, recalling our discussion of "embedded headship" from the previous chapter (regarding the role of Adam to represent God to the created order and the created order to God), in his failing and sinful

---

10. Wayne Grudem, *Systematic Theology* (Grand Rapids, MI: Zondervan, 1994), 495.
11. Jeffery, Ovey, and Sach, *Pierced*, 311–12.

rebellion, Adam has the double ignominy of introducing death and decay into the entire human race as well as the curse and frustrated groaning into all the rest of the created order.

Once again, we see a connection between human moral choices and nature. Instead of using his position of headship to mediate the blessings of God to the created order through a worshipful work of subduing and ruling, he not only experiences degradation and decay as a part of the created order but also wrongly represents the authority granted by God to subdue and rule the rest of creation, causing even worse degradations to take place.

Hardly a stewardship of worship, Adam and his descendants introduced a stewardship of futility under which the earth groans. Colin Gunton writes, "By virtue of its fallenness, the rest of the creation has lost its integrity, lost its directedness to perfection before God the Father. Though directed to an end which is perfection for the glory of God, the creation has, unaccountably but undoubtedly, fallen into disorder: that is to say, misdirection, disorientation, and dissolution." He goes on to describe this fundamental and pervasive disordering from *True North* that Adam introduced as a "deep-seated pollution . . . the result of which everything participates in an unfittedness to go into the presence of the holy God."[12] One should not take this to mean that the material creation of God is therefore corrupt and worthy of rejection. To the contrary, Scripture very clearly indicates its inherent value and "goodness." Rather, it groans in frustration from a fundamental disordering of the ones created for "embedded headship" whose leadership is now disordered and thus turns a creation that was once ordered out of chaos (Genesis 1) into orderless chaos.[13]

In this light, David Dockery's comments are both summative and on point: "Our task of living in the image of God as stewards . . . has become deformed. In human attempts to become autonomous, the man's and woman's sin resulted in the perversion of the whole order of nature in heaven and earth. The whole of creation was disrupted. The peace that existed in the garden between God, humanity, and nature was greatly disturbed." It is right to conclude, then, that "in the fall lie the roots of our ecological crisis."[14]

---

12. Gunton, *Christ and Creation*, 57.
13. For a further discussion of this, see Grudem, *Systematic Theology*, 272.
14. David S. Dockery, "The Environment, Ethics, and Exposition," in *The Earth Is the Lord's: Christians and the Environment*, ed. Richard D. Land and Louis A. Moore (Nashville: Broadman, 1992), 120.

The Tragedy of the Fall from a Theocentric Perspective

While undoubtedly real environmental degradations are taking place, given this larger context from Genesis 1–3, we trust it is now easy to see that from a theocentric perspective, such degradations are ultimately only symptoms of a far greater tragedy. The greatest tragedy in the universe is that the creation order is fundamentally disoriented from *True North*. Far and away the greatest tragedy is that God does not receive the praise and glory he is due. All other evils and injustices pale in comparison. The fact that any corner of creation (human or not) misses the opportunity to rightly glorify and praise God by pointing to and glorifying God (and thereby maximize its own existence) is simply horrific. We as humans must own the fact that the blame for this tragedy falls directly on us as willful participants in Adam's race and sinful patterns.

So in a sense, while we argued against crisis motivation in chap. 1, we now are in a position to point out that there is indeed an actual and proper way to address environmental concerns in terms of crisis language. The driving crisis, however, should not be understood in terms of degradations on nature caused by human interaction with it, nor on the more utilitarian concerns regarding possible consequences on human existence. Rather, for the Christian, the primary focus should be on the injustice relating to God and the glory he is due. This is an evil, or in the language of the environmental debate, a crisis that is clearly the single most devastating degradation of the created order that exists in the universe. It is the very thing that motivated God to rectify the situation through the incarnation and redemptive work of Jesus Christ.

III. The Gospel

As image bearers, God created human beings purposefully for relationship with himself. Thus, it is no surprise that "there is a natural longing within us for transcendence, which is grounded in God and which points to God."[15] Pre-fall, this longing was naturally fulfilled in Adam as he was aligned to *True North* and simply was "in the groove" of worshipful obedience. As we discussed in the previous section, however, although Adam was created to live in perfect relationship with God, he chose to rebel against God's eternal law and the commands he was given in the garden. As the representative head of the entire race embedded in creation to lead

---

15. Alister McGrath, *The Reenchantment of Nature: The Denial of Religion and the Ecological Crisis* (New York: Doubleday, 2002), 21.

and love it as God's "image bearer," Adam failed in the primary purpose of his existence. As Rom 5:12 indicates, instead of ushering creation into the joy of God, "through one man sin entered into the world, and death through sin, and so death spread to all men, because all sinned." Created to lead creation to *True North*, Adam instead introduced sin and death.

The "good news," however, is that while sin has positioned each person, the entire human race, and the creation itself in a state of alienation from God, God himself determined to rectify the situation. Where the first Adam failed in his primary purpose, the Second Adam would not. That is, through the person and work of Jesus Christ, the eternally divine Son of God who took on the flesh and blood of humanity, a way of reconciliation and restoration now exists.

Christ, the Second Adam (Incarnation, Recapitulation, Mediation)

The Bible clearly indicates that while Adam introduced physical and spiritual disaster into the created order, Jesus Christ's power as the "Second Adam" more than "reverses the dire consequences of the first Adam's sin, to ensure that those in him will have eternal life," and that the created order itself can be reconciled to its intended purpose and course.[16] Consider the words of Paul in Rom 5:15–21:

> But the free gift is not like the transgression. For if by the transgression of the one the many died, much more did the grace of God and the gift by the grace of the one Man, Jesus Christ, abound to the many. The gift is not like that which came through the one who sinned; for on the one hand the judgment arose from one transgression resulting in condemnation, but on the other hand the free gift arose from many transgressions resulting in justification. For if by the transgression of the one, death reigned through the one, much more those who receive the abundance of grace and of the gift of righteousness will reign in life through the One, Jesus Christ.
>
> So then as through one transgression there resulted condemnation to all men, even so through one act of righteousness there resulted justification of life to all men. For as through the one man's disobedience the many were made sinners, even so through the obedience of the One the many will be made righteous. The Law came in so that the transgression would increase; but where sin increased, grace abounded

---

16. Moo, *Romans*, 180.

all the more, so that, as sin reigned in death, even so grace would reign through righteousness to eternal life through Jesus Christ our Lord.

In this passage Paul sets up a comparison between Adam and Jesus as the two most influential individuals in history. As Schreiner puts it, this comparison is built first of all on the fact that "the status of all human beings depends on the work of Adam or Christ."[17] While they are similar in their status as representative, or "head," of the human race and the created order,[18] they are diametrically opposed to one another in regard to what they accomplished. For on the one hand, in Adam sin and death entered the world and thus "the hope of humanity for a glorious future was dashed since all of Adam's descendants entered the world under the sway of death and sin." On the other hand, Christ—through his incarnation, death, and resurrection—demonstrated his supremacy in all things by overturning all that Adam introduced into the world. As a result, the "rule over the world that Adam lost is now restored in Christ."[19] Douglas Moo comments in a similar vein that "what happened as a result of Adam's sin is entirely a matter of 'just deserts.' 'Death' . . . 'judgment,' and 'condemnation' . . . inevitably and justly follow sin. But what has happened as a result of Christ is quite different. In place of condemnation, Christ brings 'justification.'"[20]

Early in church history, the church father Irenaeus described this role of Christ as the Second Adam as a form of "recapitulation" or modified restatement of the original theme of creation. In his influential *Against Heresies*, he argued that as the representative head, Jesus Christ summed up the entire race in himself when, as the Second Person of the Trinity, He "recapitulates in Himself His own handiwork."[21] That is, "the Word, who existed in the beginning with God, by whom all things were made, who was also always present with mankind, was in these last days, according to the time appointed by the Father, united to His own workmanship, inasmuch as He became a man liable to suffering."[22]

Or as Colin Gunton eloquently puts it,

The doctrine of the incarnation states that, in obedience to the Father and through the perfecting action of the Spirit, the eternal Son comes

---

17. Schreiner, *Romans*, 282. See also Moo, *Romans*, 180.

18. Moo, *Romans*, 180. See also C. E. B Cranfield, *The Epistle to the Romans*, 6th ed. (Edinburgh: T&T Clark, 1975), 269.

19. Schreiner, *Romans*, 282–84.

20. Moo, *Romans*, 182.

21. Irenaeus, *Against Heresies* 3.22.3. and 3.22.1.

22. Ibid., 3.18.1.

in person to that realm which was made through him and which he continues to uphold. The "creative" cause of the material world comes to his own: the one through whom creation was and is formed becomes part of the creation, without ceasing to be who he is eternally.[23]

The reason Jesus took on flesh and blood and became incarnate was so he could achieve what Adam did not. Through a lifelong obedience to the Father that would ultimately result in his death, Jesus would "kill sin, deprive death of its power, and vivify man."[24]

As fully divine and fully human, Jesus Christ was born in the flesh, and as Heb 4:15 indicates, he lived a life "tempted in all things as we are, yet without sin." By living such an authentically human life without sin and fully aligned to *True North*, Jesus Christ relived the human story in a manner that redirects the wrong-headed pattern established by Adam.[25] Not only does he demonstrate the full potential of humanity unstained by sin; he is also able to understand, sympathize with, and aid the ones who call him Lord to live in a manner that is once again aligned with *True North*.

Not only is Jesus the creator of the universe, through the incarnation we see him once again stunningly affirm the goodness of the created order by humbling himself and emptying himself (Phil 2:5–11) in order to take on the living and breathing flesh of a human being. As Gunton puts it, "The one who holds in being the realms of time and space enters their confines in order to renew them. In that respect, the emptying is an expression at once of the love of the Son and of his being in relation with that which was created through and is upheld by him."[26]

The Atoning, Redeeming Death of Christ

Not only did Christ become flesh and blood to live a life of perfection as the Second Adam, he also provides through his death and resurrection the means by which the sin of Adam and all those who call upon him to be saved can be atoned for. That is, God through Christ became incarnate and assumed human nature without sin or stain so that he might also accomplish an awesome work of redemption. In 1 Tim 2:5–6, Paul clearly teaches that as the incarnate One, Jesus Christ is in the unique

---

23. Gunton, *Christ and Creation*, 79.
24. Irenaeus, *Against Heresies* 3.18.7.
25. Gunton, *Christ and Creation*, 29.
26. Ibid., 87.

role of being able to represent God to men and men to God. As such, he alone is able to mediate between God and men and even give himself as a ransom for our sins. J. I. Packer rightly describes these verses as "key" to understanding the entire message of the Bible because they so clearly indicate the central role of Christ as mediator in his work of redemption on behalf of all humankind.[27]

In his insightful little book *Christ Our Mediator*, pastor and author C. J. Mahaney helpfully spells out the human condition and the necessity of a mediator for a fallen humanity:

> Since sin has been committed by man, therefore sin must be atoned for by a man. Only a human being can be the perfect substitute for other human beings. The debt and obligation and responsibility is mankind's alone. Neither you nor I, however, can atone for our sin to satisfy God's righteous requirements; our own disobedience already condemns us before a righteous God. Furthermore, we're captive to sin; it's humanly impossible for us to release ourselves from its grip. Even if somehow, from this moment forward, we steeled ourselves to stop sinning (which is impossible), our record is still stained by the sins of our past.
>
> That's our condition—having no possible way to atone for our sin, nor any possible way to free ourselves from enslavement to it.
>
> A divine rescue is necessary. We need a savior! And in order to be our savior, in order to pay our debt, this individual must be *like us*—not just God in a form that merely appears to be human, but someone fully and truly human. Yet he must be unlike us as well, because he must be sinless, since only a perfect sacrifice is acceptable. He must be fully God, and not simply a man with a limited set of divine powers and abilities.[28]

In this light, then, we can more fully appreciate the potency of Paul's words in Rom 5:8 where he highlights the central role of Christ's death in his work of mediation: "God demonstrates His own love toward us, in that while we were yet sinners, Christ died for us." In his full humanity, Jesus perfectly represents the human race as its head (Col 1:15,18), and as such, is able to provide in himself a perfect sinless substitute for other humans who have sinned. As fully divine, he could also extend the offer of substitution infinitely to all and thus take on the fullness of all sins and receive the full wrath of God targeted at the sinfulness of all who receive him as Lord (John 1:12). Adrian Rogers nicely captures this dual

---

27. J. I. Packer, *God's Words: Studies of Key Bible Themes* (Grand Rapids, MI: Baker, 1998), 109.
28. C. J. Mahaney, *Christ Our Mediator* (Sisters, OR: Multnomah, 2004), 44–45.

role of mediation when he writes, "The Lord Jesus Christ took off His royal robes in heaven, came to earth to be born of a virgin, lived a sinless life, and died upon a cross—pouring out His rich, red, royal blood as an atonement for your sin and to satisfy the righteous demands of a holy God."[29]

The good news of Christ's redeeming work—the gospel—is this: in his death on the cross, Jesus Christ provided a full penal substitutionary atonement for human sinners and appeased the just wrath of the Father by taking onto himself the full weight and penalty of sin and in turn giving or "imputing" to those who believe and trust in Him his own status as sinless. As 2 Cor 5:21 puts it, God "made Him [Jesus] who knew no sin to be sin on our behalf, that we might become the righteousness of God in Him." Through this transaction, sinners who otherwise had no hope now experience a wondrous boon. Through his role of mediation, human beings are saved by the very person we needed to be saved from![30]

The Resurrection and Hope

In 1 Cor 15:3–4 Paul writes that it is of "first importance" not only to understand that "Christ died for our sins according to the Scriptures," but that he also was raised on the third day and eventually ascended to heaven. The reason why not only his crucifixion but also his resurrection is so vitally important is that the resurrection carries with it the promise that those who are in Christ "will be made alive" (1 Cor 15:22). The raising of Christ is representative of what will be the case for all those who are in Christ. In his *Resurrection and Moral Order*, Oliver O'Donovan develops this point well. He points out that this representation is not merely a symbol; rather, Christ's resurrection represents all believers

> in the way that a national leader is representative when he brings about for the whole of his people whatever it is, war or peace, that he effects on their behalf. And so this central proclamation directs us back also to the message of the incarnation, by which we learn how, through a unique presence of God to his creation, the whole created order is taken up into the fate of this particular representative man at this particular moment of history, on whose one fate turns the redemption of all.

---

29. Rodgers and Fox, *The Wonder of It All*, 54.
30. R. C. Sproul, *Saved from What?* (Wheaton, IL: Crossway, 2002).

Not only is this redemptive representation something that accomplishes a reality for believers in Christ now, it also has a future orientation as well. O'Donovan goes on to write that it also

> directs us forward to the end of history when that particular and repre-
> sentative fate is universalized in the resurrection of mankind from the
> dead. "Each in his own order: Christ the first fruits, then at his coming
> those who belong to Christ" [1 Cor 15:23]. The sign that God has
> stood by his created order implies that this [created] order, with man-
> kind in its proper place within it, is to be totally restored at the last.[31]

Along the same lines, 1 Pet 1:3 states that God the Father of our Lord Jesus Christ is blessed because "according to his great mercy [he] has caused us to be born again to a living hope through the resurrection of Jesus Christ from the dead." In this verse, not only does Peter indicate a physical, bodily resurrection of Jesus that affirms the goodness of the created order, it also links the resurrection to a final affirmation of the redemption and regeneration of believers in Christ. Because of this, Christians now have a "living hope," based on the historical resurrection of Jesus, not only of the reality of our salvation in Christ but of the very real future reign of the resurrected Christ who abolished death and is now seated at the right hand of the Father in glory (Heb 1:3).

Along with O'Donovan, then, we affirm that it is in the resurrection of Christ that creation is restored, and it is also in the resurrection of Christ that the fulfillment of all things is promised and assured. It is this great hope that Christians have, through the redeeming work of Christ in his crucifixion and resurrection, that becomes the basis for how we ought to think and live. As O'Donovan puts it, proper thinking about the moral life of a Christian must begin from the point that liberation was assured.[32] He writes,

> The work of the Creator who made Adam, who brought into being an
> order of things in which humanity has a place, is affirmed once and for
> all by this conclusion. It might have been possible, we could say, before
> Christ rose from the dead, for someone to wonder whether creation
> was a lost cause. If the creature consistently acted to uncreate itself,
> and with itself to uncreate the rest of creation, did this not mean that

---

31. O. M. T. O'Donovan, *Resurrection and Moral Order*, 2nd ed. (Leicester, UK: InterVarsity, 1988), 15.

32. Ibid., xv, xviii.

God's handiwork was flawed beyond hope of repair? It might have been possible before Christ rose from the dead to answer in good faith, Yes.[33]

Instead, a new and far more wonderful reality is now ushered in.

> The meaning of the resurrection, as Saint Paul presents it, is that it is God's final and decisive word on the life of his creature, Adam. It is, in the first place, God's reversal of Adam's choice of sin and death: "As in Adam all die, so also in Christ shall all be made alive" (1 Cor 15:22). In the second place, and precisely because it is a reversal of Adam's decision to die, the resurrection of Christ is a new affirmation of God's first decision that Adam should live, an affirmation that goes beyond and transforms the initial gift of life: "The first man Adam became a living being; the last Adam became a life-giving spirit" (15:45).[34]

It is from the resurrection of Jesus Christ and our identification with him in the gospel that Christians have the hope not only of new and eternal life but also of living life abundantly before God (John 10:10). Thus, it is through his death, resurrection, and ascension, Christ fully provided full atonement as the Second Adam and perfect mediator.

In sum, then, we can say that in relation to both the incarnation and the atonement, while "the former makes it possible to say that the material world's fundamental meaningfulness is demonstrated by the fact that the one through whom it took shape became material, the latter takes with full seriousness the problem of fallenness and evil."[35] By becoming incarnate and recapitulating in his own person that which he created, Jesus Christ was not only able to reaffirm the goodness of the created order, he was also able to provide redemption from sin and the opportunity for all of creation to be realigned with *True North*. Truly we can affirm with C. E. B. Cranfield "that the accumulated sins and guilt of all the ages should be answered by God's free gift, this is the miracle of miracles, utterly beyond human comprehension."[36]

---

33. Ibid., 14.
34. Ibid.
35. Gordon Lewis and Bruce Demarest, *Integrative Theology*, vol. 2 (Grand Rapids, MI: Academie, 1990), 407.
36. Cranfield, *Romans*, 286, cited from Moo, *Romans*, 183.

IV. Implications

What, then, are the implications from the redeeming and atoning work of Christ? Gordon Lewis and Bruce Demarest helpfully summarize the doctrine of atonement and state some of the more relevant implications in the following way:

> By the general term atonement, we refer primarily to the voluntary substitutionary sacrificial death of the divine-human Messiah to provide the just basis by which God could remain holy and restore peace by counteracting all the legal, experiential, relational, and cosmic effects of sin. Through faith in Christ's once-for-all substitutionary sacrifice, God can (1) acquit believers of their real guilt, (2) free them from domination by inherent tendencies to evil, (3) give them power to overcome evil principalities and powers, (4) reconcile believers to himself, and (5) reconcile them to one another.

In addition to these immediate benefits, there is also a future hope and reality. Lewis and Demarest go on to write in the same paragraph that the "future provisions of Christ's death and resurrection include (1) the provision of the incorruptible, resurrection body or the complete restoration of the divine likeness and (2) enjoyment of restored Edenic conditions in the millennium and in the new heavens and earth."[37]

Each of these identified provisions that result from Christ's redeeming work have implications for our understanding and discussion of environmental ethics. Thus, before we bring the chapter to a conclusion, there are two crucial areas we would like to focus on in the remainder of this chapter that incorporate a discussion of these points. The first is the effects of Christ's work of redemption as it relates to the rest of the visible created order. The second is the link Christ's atoning work establishes between an ethic of creation care and Christian evangelism. We will address each in turn.

The Effect of Redemption on Nonhuman Creation

In Rom 8:1–17, Paul stresses that through his redeeming and atoning work, Christ broke the power of sin and death. Therefore, for those who

---

37. Lewis and Demarest, *Integrative Theology*, 2:407. Each of these latter and future benefits will be addressed more fully in the next chapter.

are in Christ "the era of bondage to sin has ceased."[38] In addition, Paul tells us that those who are redeemed by Christ also receive the gift of the Holy Spirit, who indwells them and gives them life and strength (Rom 8:9,13). It is through the indwelling of the Holy Spirit that believers are no longer bound to follow after the sin nature they inherited from Adam. Instead, as Lewis and Demarest put it, not only are they acquitted from real sin, but they are also free from the domination of inherent sinful life patterns and choices. Indeed, Rom 8:15 tells us that because of the work of Christ, the indwelling Holy Spirit bears witness to us that we are now "adopted" as sons of God into the lineage of Christ, the Second Adam.

All of these truths are of immense importance for our discussion and understanding of creation care because they establish the baseline by which believers can now be restored into the intended purpose for which they were created. As a result, the rest of the created order has a basis for hope that it may once again receive the kind of leadership it was meant to receive from Adam before he fell into sin.

In order to understand this point it is important to recall the fact creation (that is, the nonhuman part) did not sin. According to Gen 3:17, the ground became cursed because of Adam's sin. As Rom 8:18–23 indicates, the nonhuman visible creation was then "subjected" passively to the effects of sin under which it now "groans." While the creation experiences the effects of the fall, it is not a person with the capacity for moral choice and thus it did not sin. Therefore, the nonhuman creation does not have a need of "redemption" in the same sense as human beings do. However, human beings are a part of the created order and are indeed imbedded in it. Thus, there is a very real sense in which we must say that Christ's atoning work does indeed bring redemption to the created realm; the human part of it that is imbedded in the rest of it.

While this redemption is fully accomplished in Christ, prior to the full restoration that occurs in the eschaton, when a person becomes a Christian, he or she does not immediately experience the fullness of promises that will eventually be theirs at the end of the age. However, each believer is given a new and proper position with Christ before God to pursue *True North*. As 2 Cor 5:17 indicates, "If anyone is in Christ, he is a new creature; the old things passed away; behold, the new things have come." As new creations in Christ, Paul links the believer's worshipful pursuit of God in daily life to the resurrection when he exhorts us by saying, "If you

---

38. Schreiner, *Romans*, 430.

have been raised up with Christ, keep seeking the things above, where Christ is, seated at the right hand of God" (Col 3:1). Thus, the bodily resurrection of Christ puts in place for the believer an ethical incentive to life in this world that is founded in our creation, restored by the redeeming work of Christ and which is also pulled by a future hope of bodily life in the kingdom of God. Not only should this ethical incentive push and pull us hard to avoid sin, but much more it should motivate us to pursue the very blessings God put in place "in the beginning" when he built us to worship and obey him and rule the earth in a manner that would cause the entire created order to flourish and be filled with God-glorifying creativity and culture.

So how, then, should we understand the work of redemption as it applies to the entire created realm? While we will develop this question more in our final chapter, consider the following thoughts. As we have seen earlier in this chapter, human sin and sinful patterns follow in the legacy of the first Adam and thereby negatively affect the rest of the visible created order. On the other hand, through the redemption of Christ, humans have the opportunity to be reconciled to God, adopted as his sons, and thus are placed in the legacy of Christ, the Second Adam. In a similar manner to how Adam's followers affected the environment negatively, so also should Christ's followers begin to positively reverse the effects of the fall upon the created order and affect the environment in a positive manner. By implication, those redeemed in Christ, who live under the lordship of Christ as the Second Adam, would seem to have a renewed obligation and task to reassume their role of "embedded headship" and loving dominion over the rest of creation. In this way redeemed human beings become God's agents of "re-creation" in light of the original "worship mandate" God gave to Adam in Gen 1:28.

Human redemption, then, certainly relates to the rest of creation and provides the basis for restorative work as, once again, image bearers in the lineage of the Second Adam reestablish leadership as "vice-regents" or "ambassadors" of God (2 Cor 5:21). This role is one that seeks to lovingly shepherd the rest of creation into a posture of maximizing the glory of God throughout the created realm.

It would seem, then, that perhaps more appropriate than suggesting Christ's work "redeems creation"; it would be best to understand that as "Christ's atoning work redeemed the unique part of creation that bears his image and which has been given a role of leadership among the created order," then, in and through these redeemed image bearers, the rest of creation can be called back to its created purpose and be rightly ordered or "reconciled" to God (Col 1:20).[39]

In this sense, we can understand that Jesus is not only the mediator of the original creation; his life, death, and resurrection also now becomes the basis for re-creation and the harmonizing of all things one to another and each toward God.[40] Referring back to the chart provided by Francis Schaeffer in the previous chapter, what this means is that not only do Christians have a renewed calling to be rightly related to the rest of the created order in which they are embedded, they are meant also to work hard to present the rest of the created order to God that he might be worshipped and praised. This horizontal harmonizing with the rest of creation is predicated upon the restorative work of Christ in the vertical relationship between God and man.

It is appropriate, then, to assert that by his death, the Incarnate One, Jesus, calls all of his creation back to what Colin Gunton describes as its "true destiny"[41] or as we have termed it in this book, *True North*. It is further appropriate to assert that it is redeemed image bearers—Christians—above all others who ought to be leading the way in this great, God-glorifying work of "re-creation."

Creation Care and the Great Commission (Gen 1:28 and Matt 28:18–20)

With this thought in mind, then, we believe it appropriate to review the basic flow of argument up to this point in the book to make the justification for our next point of application crystal clear. By way of review, we discovered in chap. 1 that "in the beginning" God created the heavens and the earth and that he himself is the primary point of the story. In chap. 2 we explored the meaning of Gen 2:15 where God placed Adam in the garden so that he might worship and obey. Indeed, the entire context of the Genesis creation narrative indicates that all of the created order was to function as a "temple of worship" in which those created as image bearers of God would seek to bring him glory. Not only were they to worship in Eden, in Gen 1:28 God gave to Adam and Eve

---

39. We do not mean to imply here that all elements of the curse will be reversed, as much as to argue that human contribution to it can lessen (at least) and humans can also begin to reverse the effects their sinful actions have inflicted upon it. A very simple example would be to not only stop slash-and-burn farming techniques in certain portions of the rain forest, but also to effectively engage in restorative reforestation projects.

40. Wolters, *Creation Regained*, 24.

41. Gunton, *Christ and Creation*, 122.

the command to "fill the earth, and subdue it." Therefore, it was the unique calling of Adam and Eve among all the rest of the created order to not only live a life of worshipful obedience before God, but to see to it that all of the created realm was led and shaped and ordered in such a way that the praise and glory of God would "fill the earth" (Gen 1:28).

In light of all this, it is our hope that the link between a Christ-centered, God-honoring ethic of creation care and the urgent need and responsibility for evangelism is now readily apparent.

Clearly, not only was Gen 1:28 a "worship mandate," as we suggested earlier in the book, but now we can understand that it also was a type of "great commission" in which God gave to the first human beings, and thereby all human beings, the task of filling the earth with his glory. Put another way, based on their inherent nature as image bearers, human beings are most fully human when they are both rightly aligned with the reason for which they were created and when they are rightly fulfilling the task for which they have been created. They are most fully human when they personally glorify God and seek to have the entire created order give maximum praise and honor to God. This is the *True North* for all humanity and thereby for the entire created realm.

Here, then, is the connection between an ethic of creation care and motivated evangelism for the Christian environmentalist. As God gave a great commission in Gen 1:28 to fill the earth with image bearers and subdue and rule the earth in such a way that it would bring maximum glory to him, so also does he now give a great commission to all believers to "Go" and "make disciples of all nations, baptizing them in the name of the Father and the Son and the Holy Spirit" (Matt 28:18–20). The task is the same: fill the earth with worshippers who will maximize the glory of God in their environment—all the earth!

Simply put, then, those who are most concerned about creation care and environmental justice should also *by definition* be those who are most highly motivated to share the gospel message of Jesus Christ as committed evangelists. This is so for two very specific reasons. First, human beings are a fundamental part of the created order; thus, creation care includes them. Not only does this mean a commitment to the protection of innocent human life (as we discussed earlier), but in light of the argument here, it means that caring for this part of creation in its highest form will seek to bring all human beings into a rightly ordered relationship with Jesus Christ in order that they might truly bring glory to God and in that vocation truly flourish. This form of creation care, then, requires verbal, and not just demonstrative, forms of evangelical witness.

The second reason why those most concerned with creation care and environmental justice must be motivated evangelists is more pragmatic in nature. The only hope to stop further degradations from taking place in the created order (a reality that will ultimately not happen apart from the return of Christ) is for humans to be rightly ordered to *True North*. Only then will they be able to take up the mantle of God-honoring leadership over the created order in their own lives and sphere of existence. Otherwise, environmentalism is a slave to externally imposed forms of laws and civil legislations or self-serving fear-based responses to perceived environmental crises. Both of these alternatives are vastly inferior in nature.

For the true environmentalist who understands the purposes of creation and the hope of redemption in and through Christ's atoning work, evangelism becomes the number one priority in his or her efforts to stop human-imposed degradations on the environment and in seeking the rightly ordered use and flourishing of all things created. This is not to say that he or she does not work hard in more traditional forms of environmental care. To the contrary, this is not an either/or paradigm. Rather, we believe that evangelism and more traditional forms of creation care are mutually reinforcing and synergizing in nature. The principle and long-term hope of seeing humans behave more responsibly toward the entire created realm is this: those who are created as image bearers and who have, by definition, been given headship over the created realm, will only have proper motivation and proper ordering in their efforts to guide and lovingly shepherd the creation when they are rightly related to the Creator: Jesus Christ.

Let it be clear that in asserting this point we are in no way offering some naïve pretense suggesting that "if we get 'em all saved, we'll save the planet." We clearly recognize that much debate and hard work remain both in gaining theological/ethical clarity as well as economic and political reform. For this reason we are extremely appreciative of men like Michael Northcott and Cal Beisner (to name just a few) who, although they hold very different positions on the particulars of economic theory and applied ethics related to creation care, are working hard to bring clarity and applied particulars to the discussion. Due to their training and levels of committed study, they are more able to address such issues than we are, given our limitations in those areas of expertise. Having said that, we boldly affirm that this does not change or lessen the immensity of the point we are making. If God has placed image bearers as the head of creation, and if the head is not rightly ordered, then neither will our policies be rightly ordered to the end of God-centered worship.

Ultimately, then, we see that the One who created and designed the universe to go out (*exitus*) from himself and return (*reditus*) unto him all glory also became incarnate that he might live, die, and be raised up again on Easter morning. He did this so that broken image bearers along with the entire created order could be restored to the purpose for which they were created. Jesus Christ is, then, both the foundation and the hope for environmental ethics and a properly ordered concern for creation care. From a Christocentric perspective, all efforts of creation care are predicated upon the proper ordering of all things to the purposes of Jesus Christ. Therefore, a primary (though not exclusive) task of environmental concern is the preaching of the gospel message so that image bearers designed to lead through "embedded headship" can be redeemed by God's grace through faith in Christ. Only then will they have a proper grounding and foundation to be rightly ordered to God, seek to give him glory in their own lives, and be motivated to properly order all things in the created realm to *True North*.

> God does not make junk, and we dishonor the Creator if we take a negative view of the work of his hands when he himself takes such a positive view. In fact, so positive a view did he take of what he had created that he refused to scrap it when mankind spoiled it, but determined instead, at the cost of his Son's life, to make it new and good again. God does not make junk and he does not junk what he has made.[42]

---

42. Wolters, *Creation Regained*, 49.

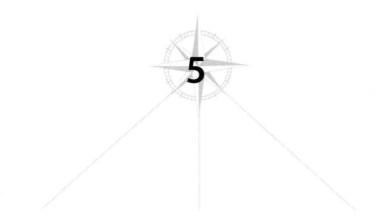

5

Eschatology—Christ the Coming King

Like all doctrines of faith, eschatology is an outworking of Christology.
God's final purpose with his creation is to "bring everything together in
the Messiah, both things in heaven and things on earth in Him" (Eph 1:10
HCSB).[1]

I. Introduction

A t the time of writing this chapter, the world symbolically celebrated the birth of the 7 billionth person on the planet Earth. A baby girl named Danica Camacho (born in the Philippines) was chosen to represent the occasion. Over the last two centuries, the rate of change in world population has increased to a stunning rate with more than 2 million people added to the population daily. These facts suggest that global population is likely to reach anywhere from 8 billion to 11 billion by mid-century. This has caused many ecological prognosticators to be concerned that planet Earth is nearing its carrying capacity, and it raises fear over the possibility of catastrophic consequences should nothing change. Questions raised about the future of our planet range from: "How long can our ecosystems sustain human consumption and waste?" and "What do we need to do as citizens of the planet Earth to ensure our survival?" to "If the Bible predicts the end of the world, why should we care about taking care of the planet?" and "Doesn't faith in Christ's return focus our hope on heaven instead of here anyway?" Underneath these various questions, we believe there lies a much more basic one: "What is the basis of hope for the future?"

---

1. Russell D. Moore, "Personal and Cosmic Eschatology," in *A Theology for the Church*, ed. Danny Akin (Nashville, TN: B&H, 2007), 893.

Up to this point in this book, we have been exploring the doctrine of Christology and its implications as they pertain to the question of caring for the environment. In chaps. 2 and 3, our discussion focused on Christ the Creator. In chap. 4, we focused on Christ the Redeemer, whose incarnation, crucifixion, and resurrection offers the one true hope of atonement for the cosmos. We now turn our discussion to the topic of eschatology and the role of Jesus Christ as the returning King who will rule and reign over all creation in an eternal future kingdom.

It is our purpose in this chapter to explore the reality of the second coming of Christ at the "Day of the Lord" and the nature of the renewal he will bring to both the created order as a whole and also specifically to his redeemed image bearers. Along the way, we will also investigate the implications of these topics for the issue of environmental ethics and creation care. Before we move on to these topics, however, we believe it first wise to put some boundaries around which aspects of eschatology we discuss, and then give some rationale for doing so.

Some Limiting Remarks: The Purpose of Eschatology in This Discussion

We wish to begin this discussion by first placing the topic of eschatology within the larger category of Christology and the plan of salvation laid out in the Scriptures. The following comment by Ken Keathley proves helpful in this regard.

> The Bible presents salvation from four perspectives: eternal, historical, present, and eschatological. First, God eternally purposed and planned our salvation before the world existed. Second, Jesus of Nazareth historically accomplished our salvation by offering his sinless life as a sacrifice upon the cross and rising from the dead. Third, we presently experience the benefits of salvation when we repent from our sins and respond in faith to the gospel message. And fourth, ultimately we will enjoy the completion of our salvation along with the transformation of all creation at the end of the age, the eschaton, when Christ returns.[2]

It is this fourth aspect, then, of the salvation work of Christ that the doctrine of eschatology attempts to come to grips with. Among evangelicals in particular, one of the more controversial and endlessly discussed

---

2. Kenneth Keathley, "The Work of God: Salvation," in Akin, *A Theology for the Church*, 695.

aspects of eschatology has to do with the timing of Christ's return and whether or how a rapture of believers might occur. On this point, Russell Moore comments that "while all orthodox Christians everywhere have affirmed the physical, bodily return of Jesus at the end of the age, contemporary evangelicals have disagreed—sometimes sharply—over the timing of this event, especially as it relates to the tribulation and the rise of the antichrist."[3] It is precisely for this reason that our discussion in this chapter will not attempt to specify dates or time periods related to the future reign of Christ.

While undoubtedly these are important areas of discussion that deserve charitable debate, we believe enough of that takes place in other venues. Further, we hold the conviction that specifications of that nature are not of central importance to *this* project. We believe it is sufficient for our purposes here to unequivocally state our belief that Christ will return and he will reign in an eternal kingdom. Our focus here is on the relevance and nature of that future kingdom to the current discussion taking place related to the creation-care debate. On this point we appreciate Moore's comment that "believers who disagree about the timing of the rapture but who hold in common the blessed hope of the second coming of Christ do not disagree on anything of central importance."[4]

In addition, for the purposes of our discussion, we would also respectfully disagree with eco-theologians like Celia Dean-Drummond who argues that "given the awesome nature of the calamity that we are now facing in terms of potential threats and real threat to the environment, a starting point for theological reflection on eschatology needs to be that of the apocalyptic," if by focusing on "the apocalyptic" she means a focus on the doom and gloom often related to future predictions.[5] While we do not want to deny the fact that Scripture speaks of apocalyptic events (indeed we will address the apocalyptic event Scripture describes as the Day of the Lord below), we also do not want to allow the discussion on eschatology and the return of Christ to be unduly colored by a sense of crisis. As Francis Bridger rightly points out, while eschatology is indeed future oriented, it need not "major on doom."[6] Indeed, from the outset

---

3. Moore, "Personal and Cosmic Eschatology," 902.

4. Ibid., 905.

5. Celia Dean-Drummond, *Eco-Theology* (London: Darton, Longman, and Todd, 2008), 164.

6. Francis Bridger, "Ecology and Eschatology: A Neglected Dimension," in *Tyndale Bulletin* 41, no. 2 (1990): 292. We found Bridger's article to be very helpful in understanding the proper place for and categories of apocalyptic language in the discussion of eschatology. In his article, he points out that apocalyptic language is often used "to denote urgency, a sense of crisis and a need to do something in order to avert the End." As such it is meant to be a catalyst for action and change. However, although eschatology is future oriented, it need not "major on doom." In fact, eschatology, when

of this book we have been at pains to demonstrate that the Christian's primary motivation for ethics is not to be based on a utilitarian calculus that seeks to justify behavior modification for fear of possible future cataclysm.

While certainly looming ecological threats ought to play a role in *catalyzing* personal and social change, they ought not to be set as primary movers of ethical action. As we pointed out in chap. 1, such forms of motivation are temporal and anemic because they fade away as the problem diminishes or becomes hopeless. For the Christian, creation care is based on the principle of ordered worship, an eternal motivation that coheres with the order of creation and the chief end of human beings. Thus, rightly understood from a Christian point of view, eschatology may include some gloomy pictures of future events, but actually, it is anything but gloomy. Indeed, when rightly understood, its aim is to push followers of Christ to understand that beyond mere condemnation (or the fear of looming cataclysms), descriptions of the end times are ultimately meant to work as a *positive draw* on our ethics as we pursue with hope the ends for which God created us from the beginning.[7]

Thus, our focus is to discuss what the Scriptures reveal to us about what the kingdom will be like when the King returns, and further, how a particularly Christ-centered approach to this topic ought to shape our view of creation care and environmental ethics.

II. The Second Coming of Christ

The Parousia

The New Testament is very clear in its proclamation that the resurrected Jesus, who ascended into heaven as Luke records in chap. 24 of his Gospel, will one day return. The Greek term for Christ's return is *parousia*, meaning "appearing" or "coming." In Acts 1, Luke records the words of heavenly messengers to the disciples as they watched their Lord bodily

---

properly understood, can even use apocalyptic language to fulfill a threefold purpose: (1) it expresses, often through symbol and imagery, a feeling, evaluation, or vision about the world; (2) it works to exert ethical pressure both on individuals and society to act in a new manner; and (3) it functions, almost by default, to condemn the current world, structure, or behavior that is addressed. See pp. 292–93.

7. This is why in his *Theological Ethics*, Helmut Thielicke comments that "theological ethics is eschatological or it is nothing." Helmut Thielicke, *Theological Ethics* (Philadelphia, PA: Fortress, 1966), 1: 47.

ascend into heaven. "They also said, 'Men of Galilee, why do you stand looking up into the sky? This Jesus, who has been taken up from you into heaven, will come in just the same way as you have watched Him go into heaven'" (Acts 1:10–11).

Thus, the biblical record indicates very clearly that when Christ returns again, his *parousia* will not only be in bodily form, but it will be in glory and triumph (Mark 8:38). First Thessalonians 4:16–17 indicates that when Christ does return, he will come descending from the sky with trumpets heralding his return along with the loud voice of an accompanying archangel.

> For the Lord Himself will descend from heaven with a shout, with the archangel's voice, and with the trumpet of God, and the dead in Christ will rise first. Then we who are still alive will be caught up together with them in the clouds to meet the Lord in the air; and so we will always be with the Lord. (HCSB)

Erickson rightly draws contrast to the first advent of Christ when he writes, "Various descriptions of the return of Christ indicate its glorious character, a sharp contrast to the lowly and humble circumstances of his first coming."[8]

When Christ does return, Scripture indicates several important realities that are tied to the event. First, his *parousia* will mark the end of life in the created order as we currently know it. Second, it will also mark the beginning of a stunning new life in the presence of the King of the universe. Third, Scripture indicates that not only does Jesus bring history to a conclusion, he will also judge the world (John 5:28–29). At his second coming, "he will sit upon his glorious throne and judge all nations (Matt 25:31–46). The irony of this situation is that he who was judged at the end of his stay on earth will be the judge over all at his second coming. Clearly, he will be the triumphant, glorious Lord of all."[9] Finally, once this has taken place, Scripture further indicates that Jesus will raise the dead, bring about their glorious transformation (Rom 8:17–18; Col 3:4), and then he will escort them into the newly transformed new creation that he will bring about.

It is for this reason that in Matt 25:36–51 Jesus tells his followers how tragic it would be if anyone were in an unprepared state when the sudden appearing of our Lord takes place. How horrible that one who is created

---

8. Millard Erickson, *Christian Theology* (Grand Rapids, MI: Baker, 1983), 1190.
9. Ibid.

in God's image to know and worship him would not be ready for the culminating experience of their entire existence!

> Scripture indicates clearly that Christ will return at some point in the future; the exact time is unknown to us. Then his victory will be complete. He will be the conquering Lord, the judge over all. At that point his reign, which at present is in some ways only potential, and which many do not accept, will be total. He himself has said that his second coming will be in glory (Mat. 25:31). The one who came in lowliness, humility, and even humiliation, will return in complete exaltation. Then indeed, every knee will bow and every tongue confess that Jesus Christ is Lord (Phil. 2:10–11).[10]

Day of the Lord

In his discussion of the second coming of Christ, the apostle Peter links the event of Christ's return to a phrase, which runs throughout the Bible, known as the Day of the Lord.

> But the Day of the Lord will come like a thief; on that [day] the heavens will pass away with a loud noise, the elements will burn and be dissolved and the earth and the works on it will be disclosed. (2 Pet 3:10 HCSB)

In the Old Testament Scripture, discussions about the Day of the Lord appear most notably in the prophetic books. As John MacArthur describes it, "The Old Testament prophets viewed the final day of the Lord as a day of unparalleled judgment, darkness, and damnation, a day in which the Lord would completely destroy His enemies, vindicate His name, reveal His glory, and establish His kingdom."[11] Some examples of its use are as follows:

> Isaiah 13:9 (HCSB) says, "Look, the day of the LORD is coming— cruel, with rage and burning anger—to make the earth a desolation and to destroy the sinners on it."

---

10. Ibid., 779.

11. John MacArthur, *2 Peter and Jude* in The MacArthur New Testament Commentary (Chicago, IL: Moody, 2005), 123–24.

Joel 2:1–2 (HCSB) indicates that all the residents of the land should tremble "for the Day of the Lord is coming; in fact, it is near—a day of darkness and gloom, a day of clouds and dense overcast, like the dawn spreading over the mountains; a great and strong people [appears], such as never existed in ages past and never will again in all the generations to come."

Zephaniah 1:14–18 (HCSB) states that "the great Day of the Lord is near. . . . That day is a day of wrath, a day of trouble and distress, a day of destruction and desolation, a day of darkness and gloom. . . . For He will make a complete, yes, a horrifying end of all the inhabitants of the earth."

Clearly, then, when Peter employs the phrase in his epistle, he is identifying the Old Testament depictions of the Day of the Lord with the second coming of Jesus Christ. In each case, there is a clear reference to a future cataclysmic event in which the world will be changed, God's judgment will be clear, and the onset and accomplishment of it would not be brought about by humankind, but by God himself. On that triumphant day, the returning King will bring to justice the individuals and nations that have defied him. He will also usher the entire created order into the peaceful flourishing that he purposed from the beginning of time.

The most pertinent question for our discussion at this point, then, is not if this event will happen (God promises it will), or even when (God tells us it is not for us to know). Rather, it seems to be, "How ought knowing that this event will take place shape our thinking about how we live, move, and worship both individually and corporately?" In light of the way Peter describes the Day of the Lord, determining an answer to that question requires that we look a bit deeper at what the coming of that day means for the created order itself.

Competing Perspectives on the Future of Creation

Following the judgment brought forth on the Day of the Lord where God will banish the wicked from the earth, Scripture indicates that God will then bring about the renewal of creation. What the nature of this new creation will be, however, is a matter under considerable debate. As one might expect, depending on where one stands on this issue, there are different perspectives on what future steps are (or are not) required of us ethically.

In his treatment on eschatology, Herman Bavinck points out that historically there has been a tendency to view discussions of the future from what he describes as two erroneous extremes. On the one hand, there are those who have a "this worldly" hope that asserts that this world is destined to continue substantially, and in form largely, as it currently is. On the other hand, there are those that tend to place an emphasis on an "other worldly" expectation that God will totally destroy the substance of this present creation and replace it with a totally new world. It is Bavinck's position—and we happen to agree with him—that "in this expectation of world renewal, Scripture assumes a position between the two extremes."[12] In order to understand this third mediating position more fully, we turn first to a discussion of the two extreme positions.

"This Worldly" Perspectives. Exploring the first of these ideas, Bavinck notes that thinkers such as "Plato, Aristotle, Xenophanes, Philo, Maimonides, Averroes, Wolanus, La Peyrere, Edelmann, and Czolbe among them—have asserted that this world is destined to continue in its present form forever."[13] Generally speaking, in more modern times, this perspective would include those who, like Ronald Sandler, adopt a more secular worldview and understand nature via scientific-naturalism.[14] Discussions of environmental ethics for someone like Sandler, then, are heavily colored by concern for the future of this planet as the "natural order" as it is our only hope for future survival.

Interestingly enough, however, it is not only scientific naturalists who fall into Bavinck's "this worldly" category. Many environmental ethicists who take a more religious perspective can be placed in this category as well. By religious, we mean very generally those who hold to some form of transcendental metaphysical understanding of the nature of the universe. Ralph Waldo Emerson's work, and the Transcendentalist movement that eventually also heavily influenced Thoreau and John Muir, is a good example of this.[15]

12. Herman Bavinck, *Reformed Dogmatics: Holy Spirit, Church, and New Creation*, vol. 4, ed. John Bolt, trans. John Vriend (Grand Rapids, MI: Baker, 2008), 716.

13. Ibid.

14. Ronald Sandler, *Character and Environment: A Virtue-Oriented Approach to Environmental Ethics* (New York: Columbia University Press, 2007), 13–14.

15. For an interesting discussion of this, see Loren Wilkinson, *Earth Keeping in the '90s: Stewardship and Creation* (Grand Rapids, MI: Eerdmans, 1991), 170–72. See also Edward Waldo Emerson and Waldo Emerson Forbes, eds., *Journals of Ralph Waldo Emerson*, 10 vols. (Boston, MA: Houghton Miflin, 1909–14), 7:241–44 and 7:511; Henry David Thoreau, *Journal, 2.4,* in *The Writings of Henry David Thoreau*, ed. Bradford Torrey and Francis H. Allen, 20 vols., Walden ed. (1906; reprint ed., New York: AMS, 1968).

In regard to the perspective based in naturalism, because there is an assumption that the matter of the universe is all there is, then, if there is no heaven, spiritual reality, or afterlife, then it is in this material universe only that we will have life and existence. Thus, preservation of this planet becomes a question of preeminent importance and our only hope of survival. The ethical motivation for such an atomistic universe is one that places hope squarely in the protection and preservation of this world precisely because it is the vessel upon which we live, and as such, the protection of it is our only hope of survival.

In the past, when planet Earth's resources were more abundant, and those competing for those resources were more scarce, questions about earth's future and human survival were more optimistic. However, with the growing number of human consumers and the increasing demands these numbers put on the varying ecosystems of the planet, there is growing concern.

Strictly speaking, from the point of view of scientific naturalism, the question of inherent value as it relates to nature would seem to be somewhat irrelevant. That is, the inherent nature of all things in a materialistic universe, by definition, is of the same inherent value, regardless of whether something is conscious (human) or unconscious (a rock). The reason for this is that without a transcendent realm, there is no basis for external differentiation to be made. In essence, the inherent value of all things is reduced to an equivalent level of that which is the lowest common denominator. Thus, because all things are made out of the same basic stuff (atoms), the value of any one thing is essentially the same as the value of any other thing.

What remains to be seen, at least from a Darwinian model of the universe, is not who or what has more inherent value, but which part of nature is "fittest." Once that is determined, there is really no basis for concern about using the rest of nature for its own ends. The reality of this morally absurd world would certainly explain the exploitation of the material world since the Enlightenment.[16] Pursuit of personal wealth would seem to have no limits, except those that come from finite ability or communal force. What, then, would cause committed materialists to limit their exploitation?

Perhaps part of the answer to this question has to do with the increasing recognition of the "web of life" and interdependent nature of all elements of the natural ecosystem. That is, as science continually demonstrates

---

16. This reality poses a serious retort to Lynn White Jr.'s claim that Christianity is at fault for the ecological crisis before us.

the interdependent nature of all the elements of the ecosystem, there is a greater awareness growing among materialists that if they want the species to survive long term, then some limitation must be placed on human consumption to ensure long-term survival. Indeed, it would seem the only limitation on this exploitation of the rest of nature would have to come from some kind of Hobbesian recognition that while all things are fair game to those who are strongest, perhaps to ensure long-term survival, some form of eco-contract needs be made between humans and the rest of nature (or at least humans and future humans) so that nature itself can survive and endure.

Former vice president and presidential candidate Al Gore's *An Inconvenient Truth* provides an excellent example of this kind of thinking. Regardless of Mr. Gore's personal beliefs, the form of argumentation is one in which survival and continuance plays the major role in moral motivation. The overwhelming focus of his work has been on what he attempted to describe as the obvious destructive behavior of human beings on their environment and the potentially (certain?) cataclysmic consequences that would result should things remain unchanged in human behavior.

Regardless of the means, the key point here is that because the hope is based on the continued existence of this world, any threat to the continuance of nature becomes a point of concern. Ethical motivation can often take the form of something like "We better do something (or anything) lest we all perish."

For others who spiritually equate nature with deity, one of the obvious differences from naturalism or a materialistic worldview is that the valuation of things within nature is considered equal, not because we are all made of the stuff of this world, but because all elements of the universe are all somehow divine. So, different from the naturalistic/materialist who would make all of nature subservient to that part of nature that is fittest, this form of thinking would argue for an equally inherent value in all things because all things equally share in the divine. Thus, the things of this world must be treated with utmost care, and no one part should hold superiority over another because all have equally inherent value.

An example of this comes in the writing of James Lovelock. In his *Revenge of Gaia*, Lovelock identifies himself and his beliefs in the following way: "There is a deep need in all of us to put our trust in something larger than ourselves and I put my trust in Gaia."[17] From this perspective, he evaluates human behavior by saying, "We are like a careless and

---

17. James Lovelock, *The Revenge of Gaia: Earth's Climate Crisis and the Fate of Humanity* (New York: Basic Books, 2007), 148. We want to be careful here to let our readers know that Lovelock's

thoughtless family member whose presence is destructive and who seems to think that only an apology is enough. We are part of the Gaian family and are valued as such, but until we stop acting as if human welfare was all that mattered, and was the excuse for our bad behavior, all that talk of further development of any kind is unacceptable."[18]

The key here is that in both these forms of argument, the ultimate hope is "this worldly." Neither is looking for deliverance from a spiritual plane or heavenly kingdom. Thus, the focus of the ethical motivation and concern is on matters related to the protection of this world. Consider Lovelock's words again. He argues that based on his evaluation of the destructive nature of human behavior, we are now facing a probable apocalyptic disaster that threatens not only human existence but also the existence of most living things. He writes, "For now the evidence coming in from watchers around the world brings news of an imminent shift in our climate towards one that could easily be described as Hell: so hot, so deadly, that only a handful of the teeming billions now alive will survive."[19] And his concern is not merely for humans. He goes on to descry the loss of "so many innocent other creatures as well."[20]

What we hope has become obvious from this discussion is that in the cultural debate about environmental ethics, there exists a strong contingency whose hope for the future is based largely, if not entirely, on the continuing existence of the world in its current substance and form. Regardless of the underlying metaphysical claims about the nature of the universe, it is the threat posed to "this world" that drives the ethical imperative to act.

"Other Worldly" Perspectives. On the other end of the spectrum are those perspectives that Bavinck categorized as "other worldly." In his highly influential work *The Travail of Nature*, Paul Santmire writes that the large majority of Christians, modern biblical scholars, and ethicists take a "spiritual motif" approach to environmental concerns. He argues that most modern Christians function in light of an excitement and focus on spiritual realities and a future kingdom of God that is so dominant that concern for the elements of this world are significantly diminished and even neglected altogether. When this "spiritual motif" drives the interpretation of Scripture, he believes, "The Pauline version of the

---

work is unique in that while claiming a worldview based largely in naturalism, his Gaia Hypothesis *takes on* a rather transcendentalist flavor in that the earth itself takes on an almost divine-like quality.

18. Ibid.

19. Ibid., 147.

20. Ibid., 148.

Christian standing in solidarity with the whole of creation at the very end is thereby eclipsed."[21]

In many cases, this more "other worldly" perspective is often reinforced by an interpretation of Scriptural passages referring to the end times that emphasize a huge discontinuity between present created order and the "new heavens and new earth." Such an interpretive motif holds that not only will the world be changed in form, but its substance will also be totally destroyed and replaced with a totally new world. Bavinck points out that such a perspective has historically been held by a wide variety of theologians, including "Origen, the Lutherans, the Mennonites, the Socinians, Vorstius, the Remonstrants, and a number of Reformed theologians like Beza, Rivetus, Junius, Wollebius, and Prideaux."[22]

In more recent times, evangelical thinkers have been influenced toward such a perspective on a popular level as it appears as the dominant idea in the popular fictional writing of C. S. Lewis in the final book of the Chronicles of Narnia series entitled *The Last Battle*. From a more scholarly perspective, this seems to be the point of view championed by what is known among theologians as "Classical Dispensationalism."

In Lewis's fictional writing, his account of the end of this world is depicted by the great lion "Aslan" (the Christ figure in the book) calling all sentient elements of creation to account and then utterly destroying all the nonsentient elements of creation. Consider these excerpts from Lewis's *The Last Battle*:

> He went to the Door and they all followed him. He raised his head and roared "Now it is time!" then louder "Time!" then so loud that it could have shaken the stars, "TIME." The Door flew open. They all stood beside Aslan, on his right side, and looked through the open doorway. . . . The creatures came rushing on. . . . But as they came right up to Aslan one or the other of two things happened to each of them. They all looked straight in his face . . . and when some looked, the expression of their faces changed terribly . . . [for some] it was fear and hatred. . . . All the creatures who looked at Aslan in that way swerved to their right, his left, and disappeared into his huge black shadow. . . . But the others looked in the face of Aslan and loved him. . . . And all these came in at the Door, in on Aslan's right.[23]

---

21. Paul Santmire, *The Travail of Nature* (Philadelphia, PA: Fortress, 1985), 217–18.

22. Bavinck, *Reformed Dogmatics*, 716.

23. C. S. Lewis, *The Last Battle* (New York: HarperTrophy, 1956), 148–54. In this and the next quote we recognize that we are citing a fictional account from a fictional world. Thus, we want to be careful to note that Lewis does not claim these views are necessarily representative of his view on this

The Dragons and Giant Lizards now had Narnia to themselves. They went to and fro tearing up the trees by the roots and crunching them up as if they were sticks of rhubarb. Minute by minute the forests disappeared. The whole country became bare. . . . You could hardly believe that anything had ever lived there. . . . Then the Moon came up, quite in her wrong position, very close to the sun, and she also looked red. And at the sight of her the sun began shooting out great flames, like whiskers or snakes of crimson fire, towards her. . . . She came to him, slowly at first, but then more and more quickly, till at last his long flames licked round her and the two ran together and became one huge ball like a burning coal. Great lumps of fire came dropping out of it into the sea and clouds of steam rose up. Then Aslan said, "Now make an end. . . ." He took the Sun and squeezed it in his hand as you would squeeze an orange. And instantly there was total darkness.[24]

In Lewis's account, once "this world" has been completely destroyed, the Christ figure in the story, Aslan, invites those persons he has rescued into a new creation that is similar in nature but perfected and more "real."

In more scholarly treatments, one can see a similar sentiment in the writings of many contemporary evangelical theologians. Here is a sampling of three evangelical scholars whose discussions related to the Day of the Lord and the future of the created order have a decidedly "other worldly" tone.

In his commentary on 2 Peter, John MacArthur comments,

In Scripture the day of the Lord signifies the extraordinary, miraculous interventions of God in human history for the purpose of judgment, culminating in His final judgment of the wicked on earth and the destruction of the present universe. . . . Peter foresaw the disintegration of the entire universe in an instant "uncreation," not by any naturalistic scenario, but solely by God's omnipotent intervention. . . . God's power will consume everything in the material realm—the entire physical earth—with its civilizations, ecosystems, and natural resources—and the surrounding celestial universe.[25]

---

matter. We simply put them here as an example of the type of thinking about the end of the world that has cache in the culture.

24. Ibid., 155–57.

25. MacArthur, *2 Peter and Jude*, 123.

John F. Walvoord arrives at a similar conclusion:

> When the Lord does come, it will be both surprising and catastrophic
> . . . the elements will be destroyed by fire . . . and the earth and every-
> thing in it will be laid bare . . . the heavens will be destroyed by fire and
> the elements will melt . . . the old cosmic system will then give way
> to a new heaven and a new earth and this is what believers are looking
> forward to, not to the earth's destruction.[26]

Tom Schriener writes in the New American Commentary that "the world
as we know it will be dissolved . . . when the day of the Lord comes . . .
the physical world as we know it will be destroyed."[27]

One can see from each of these treatments of 2 Pet 3:10 that the
conclusion reached is that the substantive elements of this world, not
merely the form and quality of them, is "destroyed" or "uncreated" and
an entirely new substantive form is ushered in.[28]

While we hold each of these men in high regard, and while we respect
their translation efforts, we are nonetheless concerned about these conclusions at this point of discussion given the nature of the 2 Peter context
from which they come. Further, we are concerned because of the possible
trajectory this perspective puts in place for creation care and other ethical
concerns. We will speak first to the latter and then expand more fully on
the former in the next section of this chapter.

Theologically and ethically speaking, Thomas Ackerman captures the
chief element of our concern in his article titled "Global Warming: Scientific Basis and Christian Responses." Ackerman comments that those
taking a perspective on eschatology that emphasizes the annihilation of
substance of this created order tend to be anti-environmentalists for a
fairly obvious reason. He writes, "If the end is near, then why would one
worry about preserving the climate of a planet that is soon to be destroyed
by the wrath of God in the giant battle of Armageddon?" Ackerman goes
on in his article to site an example of this thinking that percolates into
culture via the Internet. Again he comments,

26. John F. Walvoord and Roy B. Zuck, eds. *The Bible Knowledge Commentary* (Wheaton, IL: Victor, 1983), 887.

27. Tom Schreiner, *1, 2 Peter, Jude* in The New American Commentary, vol. 37, ed. E. Ray Clendenen (Nashville, TN: B&H, 2003), 279, 283.

28. Before offering a critique of these conclusions, we do want to point out that all three of these comments come in the context of biblical commentaries in which the authors each interacted heavily with the text of Scripture and each made strong linguistic arguments to support their case. We speak respectfully in regard to the position each of these examples represent.

In an article on his "Rapture Ready" website Todd Strandberg writes: "In 2 Peter, we are told that someday the earth will undergo a fiery renovation. All of nature and everything man has created will be completely destroyed. . . . I know that environmentalists would bristle at the idea of a refurbished earth being the ultimate solution to all ecological problems. If the world is going to be 'dissolved,' there is no need for us to become too attached to it. . . . The main job of a Christian leader is to guide lost souls to redemption. . . . In my view, any preacher who decides to get involved in environmental issues is like a heart surgeon who suddenly leaves an operation to fix a clogged toilet."[29]

We want to be exceptionally clear as we articulate our position on this point. As disciples of Jesus Christ, and as evangelicals, we are fundamentally committed to the Great Commission of Jesus found in Matt 28:18–20. Thus, we set as a priority in our lives and our call to discipleship the idea that Christians must engage culture and must set as a priority an overt, purposeful, and verbal evangelistic proclamation of the gospel message. Further, we reject the idea that setting such a priority in Christian discipleship requires, or even implies, that one set a concern for creation care (or any ethical issue) on the back burner.[30]

It is our contention here (and we will turn to that argument in the next section) that the idea that one must choose between caring for the created order and doing evangelism is not only a false dilemma, but that such thinking fosters a form of gnostic dualism in the name of Christ. Such a "Christian Gnosticism," we contend, offers a perspective on Christianity that would, even if unintentionally, deny the very goodness of the created order. It would deny the world-affirming move by God to "become flesh and dwell among us" (see John 1). It would deny the reality that Christ's resurrection and ascension was a bodily one. It would deny the validity of the future returning of Christ to rule and reign over the cosmos in the eschaton.[31]

---

29. Todd Strandberg, "Bible Prophecy and Environmentalism," accessed 12 September 2007, www.raptureready.com/rr-environmentalism.html. Cited from Thomas Ackerman, "Global Warming: Scientific Basis and Christian responses," *Perspectives on Science and Christian Faith* 59, no. 4 (December 2007): 259.

30. For a fuller discussion of some of the thinking behind this comment, please see Mark Liederbach and Alvin Reid, *The Convergent Church* (Grand Rapids, MI: Kregel, 2009), chap. 10, titled "Who's Afraid of the Social Gospel?"

31. Clearly we do not believe MacArthur, Wolvoord, Schreiner, or even Strandberg would adopt such a gnosticism. However, our concern is with the trajectory of thought and the ethical conclusions very probably related.

The danger with such a perspective is that while it rightly seeks to protect and elevate the evangelistic task set forth by Christ in the Great Commission (Matt 28:18–20) and emphasize the future hope of glory, it also devalues the creation order that God declared as good, it withers the role of proper stewardship as inherently valuable as an act of worship (1 Cor 10:31; Col 3:17), and it actually has a negative undermining effect on evangelism. This latter effect happens because such thinking devalues the instrumental evangelistic value of a life well lived as Christians live like "salt and light" before the watching world.

In concluding this discussion of what Bavinck called alternative "extreme" perspectives on the future status of this world, we believe the following insightful comments from Bruce Ashford provide a helpful summary:

> The biblical teaching concerning creation's goodness avoids the twin dangers of Gnostic dualism and idolatrous monism. On the one hand, Gnostic dualism makes a distinction between the material and spiritual aspects of God's creation, according to which the material creation is "bad" while the immaterial is "good." According to this flawed view, our bodies and indeed the earth itself are essentially bad, while our souls are essentially good. The early church, however, refuted the Gnostics, on grounds that the Gnostics refused to recognize the inherent goodness of God's creation, thereby undermining the biblical depiction of creation as well as the Incarnation and therefore the gospel itself. On the other hand, earth-lovers sometimes identify God with nature, in effect worshiping the creation along with, or instead of, the Creator. This, however, is also a clear departure from Christian doctrine. Wright argues that Christian Scripture, "while it certainly teaches respect and care for the non-human creation, resists and reverses the human tendency to divinize or personalize the natural order, or to imbue it with any power independent of its personal Creator." So the world is not bad, but neither is it God. It is God's good world.[32]

We believe that it is through understanding the link between the creation by Christ; the incarnation, death, and bodily resurrection of Christ; as well as the future restoration of the created order through Christ, that any serious disciple of Jesus Christ must reject any form of "Christian

---

32. Bruce Riley Ashford, "Creation Care Founded on the Biblical Narrative (Creation, Fall, Redemption, Restoration)," *TheoEcology* 1 (January 2012): 3. Ashford cites Christopher Wright's *Old Testament Ethics for the People of God* (Downers Grove, IL: InterVarsity, 2004), 62.

Gnosticism." Further, it is also through understanding this linking of doctrinal truths that one can recognize the immensely rich ethical motivation God has given us for all areas of ethics and certainly for caring for God's creation. Of course, our argument for the future restoration of this present created order has not yet been made, so it is to that subject we now turn.

III. The Transformation of Creation (2 Peter 3)

Of crucial importance to this discussion at this juncture is 2 Pet 3:10. We begin by citing the passage in its larger context:

> Know this first of all, that in the last days mockers will come with their mocking, following after their own lusts, and saying, "Where is the promise of His coming? For ever since the fathers fell asleep, all continues just as it was from the beginning of creation." For when they maintain this, it escapes their notice that by the word of God the heavens existed long ago and the earth was formed out of water and by water, through which the world at that time was destroyed, being flooded with water. But by His word the present heavens and earth are being reserved for fire, kept for the day of judgment and destruction of ungodly men.
>
> But do not let this one fact escape your notice, beloved, that with the Lord one day is like a thousand years, and a thousand years like one day. The Lord is not slow about His promise, as some count slowness, but is patient toward you, not wishing for any to perish but for all to come to repentance.
>
> But the day of the Lord will come like a thief, in which the heavens will pass away with a roar and the elements will be destroyed with intense heat, and the earth and its works will be burned up. (vv. 3–10)

Two elements of evaluation are necessary to understand the meaning of this text as it applies to our greater discussion of creation care. The first relates to the interpretation of v. 10 and the meaning of the phrase, "the earth and its works will be burned up." The second concerns how the context of this discussion taking place in v. 10 should be understood in light of the reference to the flood in v. 6. In other words, how ought the discussion of Noah's flood modify the interpretation of the phrase "the elements will be destroyed" in v. 10?

Meaning of Verse 10

Scholars agree it is the last clause of v. 10 that is the critical point of analysis for proper understanding. What exactly does "the earth and its works will be burned up" mean? In particular, it is the meaning of the word *heurethesetai* in the Greek, frequently interpreted to mean "burned up," that is in question.

Edwin A. Blum comments that there are three possible renderings of *heurethesetai*. It could mean that all human products will be destroyed or "burned up," which implies a total annihilation. It could also be rendered "everything in it will be laid bare," meaning that all that man does will be known in the judgment. It could also be translated as "and the earth and the works it contains—will they be found?"[33] Bouma-Prediger helps clarify why the different translation than the one we quoted above from the New American Standard Bible is possible. He writes, "The Greek verb in question here is *heurethesetai*, from *heureskein*, 'to find,' and from which we get the English expression 'eureka.'"[34] Tom Schreiner concurs, and although he takes a very different meaning from the 2 Peter 3 text than does Bouma-Prediger, he nonetheless recognizes the possibility of translating *heurethesetai* as "found." Schreiner goes so far as to comment, "We can say immediately that the external evidence decisively favors 'shall be found.'"[35]

Thus, we believe that instead of a translation that infers an annihilation of the substance of this created order (as "burned up" can imply), the text actually indicates that the earth and all its works will be "found" in the sense that they will be "found out" or "laid bare" before God. That would mean that the "intense heat" or "fire" referred to earlier in v. 10 would refer to a refiner's fire or a purging fire that burns off the dross and leaves in a purer form that which was there in the first place.

Context of Verse 6

This conclusion is further justified given the context in which this verse appears. As one can see when reading through Peter's larger discussion, he places the discussion of the world's transformation in the context of

---

33. Edwin A. Blum, "2 Peter," in *The Expositor's Bible Commentary*, ed. Frank E. Gaebelein (Grand Rapids, MI: Zondervan, 1981), 12:286.
34. Stephen Bouma-Prediger, *For the Beauty of the Earth: A Christian Vision for Creation Care* (Grand Rapids, MI: Baker, 2001), 77.
35. Schreiner, *1, 2 Peter, Jude*, 385.

the Noahic flood. Peter indicates that at that time, God "destroyed" the world through the flooding of water. Clearly, the world was not "annihilated" at that time. Its fundamental substance was not "dissolved" or done away with. Rather, it was cataclysmically destroyed. Indeed, the purpose of the flooding was to wipe out, or "purge," the evil things from the world that existed at that time. Blum notes in this regard that when God brought judgment on the planet through a flood and Noah was delivered via the ark, "the globe was not destroyed, only its inhabitants and its ordered form." Thus, he goes on to argue that when Peter makes reference to the fire, "just as in the past God purged the then-existing *kosmos* by his word and by waters, so in the future he will purge the *kosmos* by his word and by fire."[36]

Al Wolters' perspective on this passage is in keeping with Blum's in that the context of the passage is the day of judgment. That is, as the world was once judged by God with water, it will be judged again but this time with fire. With this in mind, he argues that the judgment will work as a "smelting process from which the world will emerge purified" as by fire.[37] Thus, it is not "dissolved" or annihilated but "found" in a pure form after it survives the refining fire of the smelting process.

Instead of a destruction that wipes out the substance of creation in v. 6, one should understand this to mean that there is indeed a destruction, but it is one *that affirms the continuity of the substance* of the pre-flood world and the post-flood world. Likewise, then, in context v. 10 ought to be understood as a destruction in which *the substance of the creation remains in continuity* with the world that is purged and "found," "laid bare," or revealed by a refiners fire. Russell Moore sums it up well when he says, "God does promise to destroy this present creation, but he speaks of this destruction as fire rather than water (2 Pet 3:1–13). The pre-flood creation was destroyed—the old order was wiped out. But God does not completely wipe out the earth. There is both continuity and discontinuity with the pre-flood order. The same is true of the new heavens and new earth."[38]

---

36. Blum, "2 Peter," 285.

37. Al Wolters, "Worldview and Textual Criticism in 2 Peter 3:10," *Westminster Theological Journal* 49 (1987): 408.

38. Moore, "Personal and Cosmic Eschatology," 913. See also Tom Finger's comments that reach a similar conclusion. He writes, "All evangelical eschatologies [postmillennialism, dispensationalism, historic premillenialism, and amillennialism] anticipate significant degrees of continuity between our present earth and the future world." See Tom Finger, "Evangelicals, Eschatology, and the Environment," *Scholars Circle*, monograph #2 (Wynnewood, PA: Evangelical Environmental Network, 1998), 5.

Moore goes on to comment that this continuity present in 2 Pet 3:1–10 is not merely related to an argument about the substance of the creation order; he also reminds us that this theme of continuity is present throughout the Scriptures. That is, in the same way that the substance of the creation order is maintained yet transformed in 2 Peter 3, we see that "Jesus' resurrection body is glorified and transformed, but it is still *his body*, the same body that was placed in the tomb. A regenerate person is 'a new creation' in Christ, the old is passed away (2 Cor 5:17), but he is still the same man, just transformed and redeemed."[39]

We can conclude that the text of 2 Peter, when rightly rendered, "speaks of a basic continuity rather than discontinuity of this world with the next." Therefore, we would also conclude that "creation is not ephemeral and unimportant—some weigh station until the eschaton—but rather our home, now and always. Biblical eschatology affirms the redemption and restoration of creation."[40]

Christopher Wright's comments from his *Mission of God* provide a good summary statement:

> The burden of this eschatological vision for creation is overwhelmingly positive, and this must affect how we understand the equally biblical portrayal of final and fiery destruction that awaits the present world order. . . . I prefer the textual reading of the final word in this verse that the earth "will be found." [He goes on to comment,] "I also find Richard Bauckham's interpretation of this convincing, namely, that the earth and everything in it will be "found out" that is, exposed and laid bare before God's judgment so that the wicked and all their works will no longer be able to hide or find any protection. In other words, the purpose of the conflagration described in these verses is *not the oblitera-tion of the cosmos itself* but rather the *purging of the sinful world order we live in* through the consuming destruction of all that is evil within creation, so as to establish the new creation. This fits with the previous picture of the judgment of the flood in 2 Peter 3:6–7, used explicitly as an historical precedent for the final judgment.[41]

---

39. Moore, "Personal and Cosmic Eschatology," 913.

40. Bouma-Prediger, *For the Beauty of the Earth*, 77.

41. Christopher J. H. Wright, *The Mission of God* (Grand Rapids, MI: Zondervan, 2006), 408–9. Wright cites Richard J. Bauckham, *2 Peter and Jude*, Word Biblical Commentary 50 (Waco, TX: Word, 1983), 316–22. F. F. Bruce's comments on this point also affirm this interpretation. He writes, "If words mean anything, these words of Peter denote *not* the annihilation of the present material universe and its replacement by a universe entirely new but the transformation of the present universe so that it will fulfill the purpose for which God created it. Here we have the echo of an OT hope—the creation of 'new heavens and a new earth in which righteousness dwells,' as it is put in

Now in terms of application for the Christian's perspective on creation care, we would simply point out here that because the transformation of this world is not one in which the physical matter of this world is annihilated but restored, then just as God affirmed the created order in Genesis 1, just as he affirmed it through his incarnation, just as he affirmed it through his bodily resurrection and ascension, so also does the biblical discussion of the "Day of the Lord" affirm the goodness of the substance of the created order. It is not merely good because it plays an instrumental role for human beings; it is good because God created it to be and will recreate it to be!

One should not, then, think of eschatology so much as an escape from this world but as a beautiful transformation and then proper flourishing of it.

> In the beginning God created the heavens and the earth and declared it "good." God does not surrender this good creation to Satan but wins it back through the blood of Christ, which frees creation's rulers from the sentence of death for sin (Col 1:19–21). God restores and recreates a world that vindicates his original purposes. This means not just a heavenly city of refuge for flown-away souls, but an entire universe of rocks and trees and quasars and waterfalls—everything created in which he takes delight.[42]

Further, this understanding of the created order as something good and something that God will refurbish for his good purposes flows from the fact that "this is our Father's world." That is, the creation and all that is in it belong to God, not us. As we established previously, God has appointed human beings as his regents. As such, we are to understand that this world is not ours to simply do with as we wish. It is not merely material we can exploit for gain, nor to protect at all costs because it is the "mothership" we need for survival. Nor is it something we protect at all costs because it is divine in nature. Neither extreme holds merit. Rather, the created realm is inherently valuable material because God created it, he redeems it and he will restore it, and that which he declared to be

---

an apocalyptic passage in 2 Pet 3:13, where the language of Isa 65:17; 66:22 is quoted. Apocalyptic language in which 'the heavens will pass away with a loud noise and the elements will be dissolved with fire' (2 Pet 3:10) is to be understood in the light of more prosaic statements such as Paul's and not *vice versa*." F. F Bruce, "The Bible and the Environment," in *Living and Active Word of God: Essays in Honor of Samuel J Schultz*, ed. Morris Inch and Ronald Youngblood (Winona Lake, IN: Eisenbrauns, 1983), 29; emphasis added.

42. Moore, "Personal and Cosmic Eschatology," 913.

good prior to the fall he still values now and will into the eschaton. Our use of it, then, must be on his terms, and we must honor it in a manner that he would be pleased with. In relation to our discussion here of God's renewal of the creation, we can conclude that his future renewal of creation places a current demand on us to treat it well. As my parents always used to tell me as a child when we used something that did not belong to us: "It is our responsibility to return it to the owner in better shape than we got it." We believe the same idea applies here.

But even if one was not persuaded by our argument here regarding the interpretation of 2 Pet 3:10, it is still important to point out that even if God were to burn up this world and annihilate the matter it is made of, such a reality would still not authorize any one person or humanity as a whole to merely use it instrumentally as we wish. Given the commands of God and his own proclamation of ownership of the world, even if *he* decides to totally annihilate this present world, it does not follow that any Christian obedient to the lordship of Christ could justify *our* destroying it. Such an argument would be a serious presumption on God's grace and a denial of his commands. Bouma-Prediger makes this point forcefully when he says, "It is a non sequitur to argue that because the earth will be destroyed in the future, humans, therefore, should exploit it in the present. To use an analogy, is it permissible for me to plunder your house just because some time in the future it will be torn down? The fact that something will eventually be destroyed gives no license to abuse or neglect it."[43]

Placing these conclusions in the larger scope of what we are trying to accomplish in this chapter, then, we would affirm that when the "Day of the Lord" arrives and the Lord Jesus Christ comes again to judge the living and the dead, the renewal of creation will follow the final judgment. Then, according to the Scripture, "the present world will neither continue forever nor will it be destroyed and replaced by a totally new one. Instead it will be cleansed of sin and re-created, reborn, renewed, 'made whole.' While the kingdom of God is first planted spiritually in human hearts, the future blessedness is not to be spiritualized."[44] Thus, just as the creation by God in Genesis is world affirming, and just as the incarnation and resurrection of Christ are world affirming, so also will the restoration or re-creation of this world be world affirming. The key to this all is the person and work of Jesus Christ, who was and is and is to come.

---

43. Bouma-Prediger, *For the Beauty of the Earth*, 78.
44. Bavinck, *Reformed Dogmatics*, 715.

IV. Bodily Resurrection and the Eschaton

In addition to the fact that God in Christ will transform the present world, Scripture is also clear that humans are a part of the created order, and we also will be transformed by the grace of God. That is, the Bible also teaches us that when Christ Jesus redeemed us, his work on our behalf was not merely one that resulted in the salvation of our souls but of our whole selves—body and soul. Indeed, the testimony of Scripture draws a clear link between both Jesus' bodily resurrection and ours. For example, in 1 Cor 6:14 (HCSB), Paul writes that "God raised up the Lord and will also raise us up by His power." But not only is our bodily resurrection accomplished by the resurrection of Christ, Scripture also attests that "the rebirth of human beings is completed in the glorious rebirth of all creation, the new Jerusalem, whose architect and builder is God himself."[45]

Jesus' Bodily Resurrection and Ours

Without a doubt, the entire canon of the New Testament bears witness to the bodily resurrection of Jesus, recorded specifically in the Gospel accounts of Matthew 28, Mark 16, Luke 24, and John 20–21. Scripture also makes clear that Jesus' resurrection body was indeed a physical one. This reality is also clearly demonstrated through the Gospel accounts of his post-resurrection encounters with the disciples. In Matt 28:9, the disciples touch his feet. Luke indicates that Jesus took bread and broke it in the presence of his followers (Luke 24:30). John records that Jesus ate fish (John 21:15) and that he prepared a meal for his disciples (John 21:12–13).

We must be careful, however, to understand that Jesus' resurrection was not merely a "coming back to life" or a resuscitation of a broken crucified body. Scripture attests to the reality that in addition to his body being resurrected, Jesus' humanity itself was transformed. What took place that Easter morning was "the creative renewing of his original body, the body that is now fully glorified and deathless (Phil 3:21; Heb 7:16,24)."[46] At the resurrection, Jesus "put on immortality" (1 Cor 15:53). His resurrection body took the form of what Paul calls in 1 Corinthians 15 a "spiritual body" (v. 44).

---

45. Ibid.
46. J. I. Packer, *Concise Theology* (Carol Stream, IL: Tyndale, 1993), 125.

As Paige Patterson points out, it is important to understand that the terminology "spiritual body" is something of an anomaly. For in the Greek mind, the two words "spirit" and "body" were almost inevitably viewed as mutually exclusive. However, when Paul uses the term in 1 Corinthians 15, he "is affirming that there is, in fact, an entity that is authentic and observable, yet it exists in an incorruptible, glorified state that can only be described as 'spiritual.'"[47]

If, then, Jesus' body was a "spiritual body," how then can it also be "physical" as these Gospel accounts attest? Grudem offers a helpful discussion. When Paul uses the term "spiritual body," he "does not mean 'immaterial,' but rather 'suited to and responsive to the guidance of the Spirit.' In the Pauline episodes, the word 'spiritual' (Gk. *pneumatikos*) never means 'nonphysical' but rather 'consistent with the character and activity of the Holy Spirit' (see, e.g., Rom 1:11; 7:14; 1 Cor 2:13,15; 3:1; 14:37; Gal 6:1)."[48]

Grudem goes on to clarify this thought by offering a helpful paraphrase to the above cited 1 Cor 15:42–44 passage. He writes, "It is sown a natural body subject to the characteristics and desires of this age, and governed by its own sinful will, but it is raised a spiritual body, completely subject to the will of the Holy Spirit and responsive to the Holy Spirit's guidance." Commenting further, "Such a body is not at all 'nonphysical,' but it is a physical body raised to the degree of perfection for which God originally intended it."[49]

What is the point and importance of this discussion as it relates to eschatology? As 1 Pet 1:3 indicates, we have been "born again to a living hope through the resurrection of Jesus Christ from the dead." This means, at least in part, that "the physical resurrection of Jesus, and his eternal possession of a physical resurrection body, give clear affirmation of the goodness of the material creation that God originally made: 'And God saw everything that he had made, and behold, it was very good' (Gen 1:31)."[50] This is the point we have demonstrated in the previous chapter in our discussion on Christ the Redeemer. This is not, however, all we can learn from the 1 Pet 1:3 passage. It also indicates that an important connection exists between the resurrection of Christ and the future resurrection of the believer.[51]

---

47. Paige Patterson, *The Troubled and Triumphant Church* (Eugene, OR: Wipf and Stock, 2002), 302.

48. Wayne Grudem, *Systematic Theology* (Grand Rapids: Zondervan, 1994), 609 n. 3.

49. Ibid.

50. Ibid., 613.

51. Romans 8:11 also affirms this point. "But if the Spirit of Him who raised Jesus from the

The resurrection of Christ is an assurance of a promise that in the eschaton believers will also be raised by the same power that raised Christ from the dead. Not only this, but also that like Jesus, our resurrection will be bodily as well. This is why throughout the ages of the church, regardless of the denomination to which one might belong, Christians have been taught (through the Apostles' Creed) to say, "I believe in the forgiveness of sins; the resurrection of the body; and the life everlasting." Just for clarification, this bodily resurrection is one that will be a resurrection of our current bodies. Indeed, the whole idea behind the word "resurrection" is a living again of that which was dead. Resurrection implies continued identity "not of something of the same nature, but the very thing itself."[52]

Some of our readers may find themselves saying at this point (as I am), "If it is this body that is going to be raised, I am not sure I am excited about it." Not to worry; Scripture implies that an extreme makeover will take place for all of us! Indeed, it is the promise of Scripture. Philippians 3:21 affirms this in telling us that, like Christ, our bodies will also undergo a glorious transformation:

> He will transform the body of our humble condition into the likeness
> of His glorious body, by the power that enables Him to subject every-
> thing to Himself. (HCSB)

Therefore, while it is certainly the case that our bodies in their current state are not adapted to our future state of existence, Paul, in essence, is recognizing that what is currently corruptible must (and will) be transformed into something incorruptible; that which is perishable will be made imperishable (1 Cor 15:42). It is, then, through the eschatological transformation of our bodies (as it also was for the created order itself) that we see yet again an affirmation of the world God originally created. Paige Patterson writes: "In I Cor[inthians] 15 continuities and discontinuities between old and new are set forth such that the reader can be left in no doubt that the Resurrection of Christ heralds not only humanity's future resurrection but the vindication of the whole created order."[53]

---

dead dwells in you, He who raised Christ Jesus from the dead will also give life to your mortal bodies through His Spirit who dwells in you."

52. Charles Hodge, *Systematic Theology*, vol. 3: *Soteriology* (Peabody, MA: Hendrickson, 2003), 774–75.

53. Patterson, *The Troubled and Triumphant Church*, 302. See also Grudem, *Systematic Theology*, 613. Grudem comments, "In this very material, physical, renewed universe, it seems that we will need to live as human beings with physical bodies, suitable for life in God's renewed physical creation. Specifically, Jesus' physical resurrection body affirms the goodness of God's original creation of

Resurrection and the Restoration to *True North*

One of the grand implications from all that we have addressed so far in this chapter is that in the transformation and restoration of the created order, we find not only the return to beauty, but also the re-establishment of moral/spiritual purpose, or telos, of all creation. Consider the words of Oliver O'Donovan on this point. In his influential *Resurrection and Moral Order*, O'Donovan writes,

> The resurrection carries with it the promise that "all shall be made alive" (1 Cor 15:22). The raising of Christ is representative, not in the way that a symbol is representative, expressing a reality which has an independent and prior standing, but in the way that a national leader is representative when he brings about for the whole of his people whatever it is, war or peace, that he effects on their behalf. And so this central proclamation directs us back also to the message of the incarnation, by which we learn how, through a unique presence of God to his creation, the whole created order is taken up into the fate of this particular representative man at this particular moment of history, on whose one fate turns the redemption of all. *And it directs us forward to the end of history when that particular and representative fate is universalized in the resurrection of mankind from the dead.* "Each in his own order: Christ the first fruits, then at his coming those who belong to Christ" (15:23). The sign that God has stood by his created order implies that this order, with mankind in its proper place within it, *is to be totally restored at the last.*[54]

Here O'Donovan draws out that not only does the bodily resurrection of Christ affirm the created order, but because Christ is also the head of all creation, his resurrection also restores the created order to the intended purposes God has for it. What this means for us is that, far more than a hope of personal resurrection at the *parousia*, that resurrection is one in which the entirety of the cosmos will also be transformed

---

man not as a mere spirit like the angels, but as a creature with a physical body that was 'very good.' *We must not fall into the error of thinking that nonmaterial existence is somehow a better form of existence for creatures: when God made us as the pinnacle of his creation, he gave us physical bodies.* In a perfected physical body Jesus rose from the dead, now reigns in heaven, and will return to take us to be with himself forever" (emphasis added).

54. O. M. T. O'Donovan, *Resurrection and Moral Order*, 2nd ed. (Leicester,UK: InterVarsity, 1988), 15; emphasis added.

back into an incorruptible moral and spiritual trajectory toward *True North*.[55]

Very specifically in relation to eschatology, then, if we keep Wayne Grudem's discussion about the nature of spiritual bodies in mind, we can say that the resurrection of Christ and the promised resurrection of all who have died in Christ is a physical resurrection to a future restored and transformed physical world. Its "physicality" is not of the same it is now; rather, it is a physical world that is consistent with the character, activity, and teleological purpose of Christ.

Restored Headship

In this light, then, we can see also that the implications of our bodily resurrection into a future transformed new creation also includes the realization that humans will once again be able to fulfill their specific role given to them by God at creation: headship. First John 3:2 (HCSB) gives us some important insight into this point. The apostle writes, "Dear friends, we are God's children now, and what we will be has not yet been revealed. We know that when He appears, we will be like Him, because we will see Him as He is." We believe this transformation not only to be one of bodily change, but of moral change in which the longings, desires, and will of God's children will also be properly aligned once and forever toward *True North*. The One who was the author of our faith now becomes the perfect finisher of our faith (Heb 12:2). The one who began a good work in us will on that day bring it unto completion (Phil 1:6).

Because of this total and perfect recalibration of each one's moral compass, we will experience the joy of moral restoration in Christ to the position God originally created for us to hold. In the eschaton we will be able once again to share in the authority of Christ over the entire new creation. What is positionally true now in the gospel will be fully realized in the eschaton. That is, Eph 2:4–9 indicates that we have been co-raised with Christ and co-seated with him in the heavenlies where he sits at the right hand of the Father. This positional truth based on the work of Christ on our behalf in the gospel is also the indicator of our future restored place of dominion over the created order.[56]

---

55. Moore, "Personal and Cosmic Eschatology," 860.

56. Grudem, *Systematic Theology*, 619. See also Erickson, *Christian Theology*, 997. As the Apostle's Creed states this doctrinal reality: "On the third day he rose again; he ascended into heaven, he is seated at the right hand of the Father, and he will come to judge the living and the dead."

This seems at least in part to be the sense of why "the creation itself will also be set free from the bondage of corruption into the glorious freedom of God's children" (Rom 8:21 HCSB). For while the world did not sin yet was subject to futility, now with the restoration of image bearers in Christ, the entire cosmos can experience freedom from futility as a God thrilling, nonfallen dominion is restored in a new creation where image bearers maximize their expressions of worshipping and glorifying God in a new creation they shepherd to do the same.[57]

---

57. Erickson, *Christian Theology*, 1001.

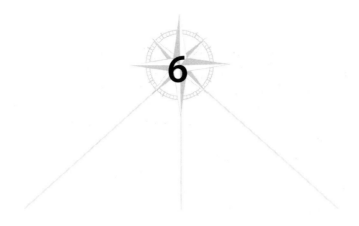

6

True North Pursued

Man's life on earth is important to God; he has given it its order; it matters that it should conform to the order he has given it. Once we have grasped that, we can understand too how this order requires of us both a denial of all that threatens to become disordered and a progress towards a life which goes beyond this order without negating it.

O. M. T. O'Donovan[1]

I. Introduction

We began this study with a discussion of power and the importance of worldviews in shaping and directing the way we express power. Citing a discussion from the insightful works of James Davidson Hunter and Al Wolters, we pointed out that power is a human facility that is used to shape and direct our world. While it is not self-directing, power does move things in a direction depending upon the moral compass or worldview of those people and social institutions that wield it. Obviously, then, the basic convictions and fundamental ideas that shape a worldview are all important. Indeed, ideas have consequences.[2]

Our discussion then pointed out that there are two prominent streams of thought in our culture vying for supremacy in the environmental debates of our day. Both streams propose a particular methodology (which are often at odds) as to what direction our energies should be spent in order to address the presenting concerns about the environment

---

1. O. M. T. O'Donovan, *Resurrection and Moral Order* (Leicester, UK: InterVarsity, 1988), 15.
2. For a full discussion of this concept, see Richard M. Weaver, *Ideas Have Consequences* (Chicago, IL: University of Chicago Press, 1948).

and the ability of planet Earth to sustain the increasing levels of consumption and pollution. On the one hand, there are those who believe there is a very real and impending ecological cataclysm on the horizon. That probability demands our immediate action (for some, by whatever means necessary) if we are to avert disaster, or at least mitigate its impact. On the other hand, there are those who deny the urgency of the matter either because they are fundamentally skeptical that such a disaster is looming or because they have such a high regard either for supernatural rapture or technological deliverance. The first group we nicknamed "Chicken Littles," the second "Ostriches."

Ultimately we believe both of these approaches are wrong. Let us be clear to say that we are not suggesting they are unimportant. The fact of the matter is that they are vitally important. The reason we say they are wrong is that they are focusing on the question What should we do? before having established clarity on the questions Why should I care? and How should I think? As important, and as pressing, as the *what* questions are, our experience (both in personal interactions with laity and public interactions at national conferences) shows a tremendous lack of clarity (even among theologically trained Christians) as to the *whys* and *hows* that must undergird and shape the *what* questions. So perhaps it would be fairer of us not to say they are "wrong" but rather "out of proper order."

No doubt, part of the reason for this is the sense of urgency that has been thrust upon us by intense and constant public expressions of concern about impending doom and cataclysmic environmental disasters. We understand this. It is far better, we believe, to first ask where we are going and how should we get there before everyone jumps in the boat, shoves off, and starts rowing. As much as we would like to say or believe that the basic direction and skills are already in place, experience teaches us otherwise.

This is why in this book we have not addressed particulars of economic, political, or social structures. It is not that we believe they are unimportant or that we naïvely think that if we get everyone to love Jesus, we can just expect everything to work out. Such Pollyannaish thinking is ridiculous. No, it is our task to lay the foundations biblically and theologically so that we can *rightly* move into discussions of particulars about economic, political, and social structures.[3]

---

3. Indeed, anyone who disagrees with this is either intensely naïve to the potency of fundamental ideas or they are naïvely overconfident in the basic structures of thought that shape prevailing worldviews in our culture.

Those goodhearted leaders among the Chicken Littles and Ostriches who love Jesus and want to do what is right for this world, must not assume that the average folks they are trying to lead have an adequate understanding of the fundamental doctrines of their faith. All of us must work hard to understand our basic faith commitments and humbly but aggressively shape our worldview according to Scripture if we are to have any hope of directing the flow of our power and the motions of our efforts toward *True North*. Colin Gunton captures this thought well.

> The danger of much recent theology, especially that forming the life of the churches today, is that it will be so dominated by activism—with churches doing things, changing the world, achieving justice, etc.—that we shall forget that at the centre of both Old and New Testament concerns is the matter of teaching. The first source of the renewal of the image, the reshaping of human directedness, is a sitting under the word which is the representation, actualizing indeed, of the story of the Word incarnate; in the words of Colossians, "being renewed in knowledge after the image of the creator" (Col 3:10).[4]

It is our mission in the remainder of this chapter, then, to accomplish two tasks. First, we will provide a summary review of the argument up to this point. Then we will offer a brief discussion on "How we should think" before bringing the book to conclusion. Once again, if it is true that God created the world and called it good, if he redeemed it, and if he seeks to restore and transform it so that all of creation can glorify him forever, then ultimately we are on a journey of worship as we pursue *True North*. Thus, ours must be an ethic of worship in which the people of God seek conformity to Christ through obeying the commands of his revealed Word. We will develop these ideas more fully below, but first, a review and summarization.

II. Review and Summarization

In his work *Nature and Altering It*, Duke professor of Christian ethics Allen Verhey writes,

> Christian ethics proceeds "by way of reminder." That is just to follow the example of Paul, who wrote to the Roman churches "by way of reminder" (Rom 15:15). He reminded them of "the gospel of God"

---

4. Colin E. Gunton, *Christ and Creation* (Grand Rapids, MI: Eerdmans, 1997), 112.

(1:1) in order to bring about "the obedience of faith" (1:5; 16:26). The first rule for Christian ethics ought always to be "Remember! . . . Christians read Scripture in order to remember, and that memory is constitutive for identity and determinative for discernment."[5]

It has been our argument from the beginning of this project that the central point of this "remembering" Verhey speaks of is the person and work of Christ revealed by the Scripture as the Alpha and the Omega, the Beginning and the End, and the Author and Finisher of our faith. This has been for us the operating principle behind the metaphor of *True North*. Thus, throughout this book we have argued that as the Creator, Redeemer, and returning King, Christ—the Second Person of the Trinity—is both the means to, and object of, pursuing *True North*.

Thus, while this book has ostensibly been a book about environmental ethics and creation care, we are sure by now our readers understand that it has really been primarily a study of Christology. From the beginning, our assumption has been that we can only rightly determine *how* to live and *what* to do in this world after we have studied *who* it is that made the world, and *why* he set it in motion. Thus, we have been seeking to make application from the study of God in Christ to the world of ethics and action.

Our journey, then, has been an exploration of the Scriptures as both revealed reality and revealed morality. That is, we have been searching the Word of God as our chief source of authority in order to discover what has been revealed to us not only about the nature and purpose of creation but also about the implications of those things for daily life on this planet. The argument we have made can be summarized as follows.

First, we began our journey by studying the opening words of the Bible and Paul's Christological discussion in Colossians 1 to discover that God himself is *True North*. Contrary to any reading of the creation narrative that would place the creation as the center point of the story, a proper reading clearly indicates that God is meant to be the focus. All things were created *by* Jesus Christ, the Second Person of the Trinity, and as such, they were also created *for* him. It was designed by God to flourish unto the glory of God.

Next we explored the special and unique privilege God gave to humans as image bearers and the unique responsibilities that go with such a position. As God's special agents who are embedded in the created order, humans are tasked with responsible leadership. This God-honoring

5. Allen Verhey, *Nature and Altering It* (Grand Rapids, MI: Eerdmans, 2010), 63.

"headship" was never meant to be one of self-oriented, exploiting domi-
nance. Rather, it was meant to be a position of vice regency, stewardship,
and shepherding in which those given authority by God would use their
gifts and talents to forcibly shape the world into an expansive and ever
increasingly beautiful sanctuary of worship. They were created, embedded, and empowered by God to lead in his name and in a manner that
would honor and thrill him. Every aspect of life, every particle of matter,
every sector of the universe was to be ordered unto God without guilt,
shame, sorrow, or flaw.

Third, we demonstrated the unfortunate reality that human beings
did not stay on this path toward *True North*. Instead, all of us went
our own independent way and rebelled against God and his eternal
law. This deviation (or depravation) from *True North* is what the Bible
describes as sin. Humans chose a course of action that not only caused
them to be cast out of the garden, but most importantly, it caused a
break in relationship with God. They fell. And the wages of that fall
was (and is) death—a spiritual separation from God, and life in an
environment that was cursed because of them and would forever groan
for redemption.

Fourth, we showed from Scripture how against all hope, and only by
a gracious and merciful act of God, redemption came in the person of
Jesus Christ. In the Second Person of the Trinity, God himself became
incarnate and was born as a human being who would live a sinless life
and die on a cross in order to bear the sins of the fallen world. Those
who would accept this plan of salvation and place their faith and loyalty
in him could have a restored relationship with him once more. But not
only did he die to offer a penal substitutionary atonement for sinners,
his bodily resurrection and ascension into heaven confirmed his divine
position as the Redeemer of all things, as well as once again affirming the
goodness of created matter. That salvation and reversal of the curse has
been fully inaugurated in Christ, but the final consummation awaits a
future day when the Lord returns.

Finally, we saw that at the "Day of the Lord," Scripture teaches that
Christ will bodily return to judge the living and dead as well as to bring
a wondrous transformation to the entire created order. On that day, he
will usher in the new heaven and the new earth. On that day, he will
fully transform the resurrection bodies of all the redeemed image bearers
of God. On that day, he will also bring full, complete, and permanent
restoration of the entire cosmos to its created directional trajectory. As it

was created to be in the beginning, so it shall be in the end: the entire cosmos will be rightly aligned and will forever joyfully pursue *True North*.

Scripture teaches that not only does God create the universe and call it good, he also incarnates himself into it, bodily resurrects and ascends from it, bodily returns to it, and then brings actual, material transformation and restoration of it. God saw what he had made and it was good! God sees what he has made and it is good! God will see what he transforms and it will be wholly good forevermore!

This is the reason *why we should care* about every aspect of life. In specific relationship to the topic of environmental ethics and creation care, it is the reason we care *about* and *for* creation. Ultimately, the lordship of Jesus Christ demands it. This notion can be summarized in the following way:

- We care because God made it. That is, we take care of his stuff (Gen 1:1).
- We care because he asked us to. That is, we are responsible for it (Gen 1:28).
- We care because he cares. That is, we love what he loves (Gen 1:31).
- We care because he put us on a mission. That is, he told us to fill the earth and subdue it (Gen 1:28).
- We care because when we care, he is most glorified. That is, he told us to worship and obey and fill the earth with worshippers (Gen 1:28; 2:15; Hab 2:14; Matt 28:18–20).
- We care because he redeemed creation (Romans 8).
- We care because he is coming again to transform creation (2 Pet 3.10).
- We care because he will live and reign with us in the newly transformed creation (Revelation 21–22).
- We care because he commands us to conform to his image and imitate him (Rom 8:29; 1 Cor 11:1).

To adequately close this section, we offer this quote by Bruce Ashford that we believe correctly summarizes this list:

> This is the doctrine of creation come full circle. The good God who called us to be stewards of his good creation, who promised redemption in light of man's sin, is the same God who will restore his creation, bringing forth a new heavens and earth unblemished by sin and its consequences. This narrative, with creation and restoration as its

bookends, provides the framework for a Christian theology of environmental stewardship.[6]

III. How, Then, Shall We Live?

Obviously, conformity to his image places a massive demand on our lives. But this is the cost of discipleship, and it is the path to joyful flourishing. It can only happen as we: (1) keep his grand scheme in front of us, (2) seek to conform ourselves to Him, and (3) obey him, through the power of the Holy Spirit and careful attention to his Word in order to conform ourselves to Him. Even then, Scripture teaches us, our striving for it now will only take on wholeness when we see him face to face (Phil 1:6; 1 John 3:2). This conclusion, then, brings us to the obvious question: How, then, shall we live? It is to that topic we now turn.

Keeping His Grand Scheme in Front of Us:
The Compelling and Alluring Power of Christ

In chap. 2, we discussed the basic exit- and return-pattern of the universe that in Latin is rendered *exitus et reditus*. Now that we have worked through our theological discussion and have seen the fullness of this pattern expressed through the doctrines of creation, fall, redemption, and restoration, we trust it is not a difficult step to see that this basic exit- and return-pattern should also function as our structure of ethics.

In short, we have argued that the universe, everything and everyone in it, was created by God and for God's own glory.[7] As created beings who have been given the status as image bearers and the responsibility of "embedded headship," God gave us the task of going forth in his name in order to see that the entirety of creation would bring back unto him all the honor and glory the created order could muster.

As we discussed in chap. 3, image bearers were created to be, and by ontological design are, constant worshippers (Gen 2:15; Isa 43:7). Therefore, by the very nature of how God created us and because of

---

6. Bruce Riley Ashford, "Creation Care Founded on the Biblical Narrative (Creation, Fall, Redemption, Restoration)," *TheoEcology* 1 (January 2012): 6.

7. As Jonathan Edwards rightly affirms in his classic work *Concerning the End for Which God Created the World*, the glory of God is the chief end of *everything*. See sections 2.3.142; 2.4.221; 5.10.238–9; 7.264–285. See also Charles Hodge, who affirms this idea when he states, "The final cause of all God's purposes is his own glory" (*Systematic Theology* [Grand Rapids, MI: Hendrickson, 2003], 1:535).

the position he placed us in, it is proper to understand that *by definition* human beings are worshippers and *by calling* we are to be "worship leaders" among the created realm. Because the indicative is that we are worshipping, the imperative for us is to worship well and lead well in all that we do (1 Cor 10:31; Col 3:17).

Based on these ideas, then, we assert that the entire trajectory of creation, including the very fabric and orientation of human life, is one of worship. Humans were created to perfectly worship God in complete harmony with one another, the heavenly host, and even the nonsentient creation. This worship orientation was fundamentally and necessarily linked to the actions, behavior, motivations, and goals of all human beings. That is, ethics and worship were intentionally and integrally united by the Creator. *Exitus et Reditus.* Everything was created *by* him and *for* him. Thus, the gospel of Jesus Christ, in addition to redeeming us and providing atonement (discussed in chap. 4), also restores us to a position from which we can rightly worship God "in spirit and truth" (John 4:20–24). As his redeemed image bearers, we are to do this individually, corporately, and on behalf of the created order we are called to rightly order and lead. This is the doctrine of sanctification.

Now if all this is true and we have properly expressed the trajectory of the gospel story from the very beginning, then clearly for Christians, Christ himself is both the source and object of our hope that is to determine the impulse, shape, and direction of our ethics.

This is why Tozer reminds us that "what comes into our minds when we think about God is the most important thing about us."[8] It is why Bonhoeffer was correct when he asserted that the fundamental question of Christian ethics is always one that addresses *who* prior to *how*.[9] You see, our thoughts about God, and our understanding of who he is, play the determinative role in our motivation for ethics. If our view of God is small and unworthy, then the motivation to obey and the desire to return our lives and world unto him will be tepid.[10] Frequently, other things will tempt us and draw us away from proper worship. For example, in relation to our discussion of the environment, Michael Northcott rightly points out that worship, whether it is rightly or wrongly ordered,

---

8. A. W. Tozer, *The Knowledge of the Holy* (New York: Harper Collins, 1961), 2.

9. Dietrich Bonhoeffer, *Christology* (London: Collins; New York: Harper & Row, 1966).

10. Of course, this is completely distasteful to God. See Rev 3:15–16. For a further discussion on this, see J. B. Phillips's classic little devotional *Your God Is Too Small* (New York: Touchstone, 2004).

is at the heart of our ecological crisis. It is precisely the modern devotion to the cult of consumerism which is driving the horrific global scale of environmental destruction. The modern western appetite for a constant and changing flow of consumer goods represents a spiritual disease, and is indicative that Western civilization has at its heart a devotion to that which is not God. "Idolatry" is the word used in the Old Testament to describe the worship of created things in the place of God. And idolatry is wrong, not only because it displaces the worship of God with the worship of that which is not God, but also because the worship of these non-gods, or idols, is itself a source of evil.[11]

If, on the other hand, our vision of God reflects who he really is—a vision as expansive and beautiful as the universe (indeed even grander and more stunning)—then the impulse of the moral life will be massive and powerful. The lesser gods of this world and culture hold less sway, and the motivation of our ethical life before God shifts from mere duty to delight. Image bearers eagerly go forth to please their Creator, and they eagerly seek to return and hear their future coming King say, "Well done!"

Thinking from creation, redemption, and eschatological categories, then, results in a form of ethics that is both compelling and alluring. There is a type of "push-pull motivation" that emerges in the life of the believer. Not only are human beings created as worshippers who eagerly go into their environment and use their gifts and talents to expansively co-create with God a culture that seeks to cause all of it to flourish before the Lord, but the future certainty of the promises of God function with a certain magnetism that pulls us through our actions to worship our Savior. The beauty of the eschatological kingdom has an alluring power that coaxes us toward the One who promises it.

Between the times, then, the mandate of creation and the hope of consummation pushes and pulls on our ethical motivations at the same time to create a motivated holiness that must express itself in the lives of believers, individually as well as part of the corporate body of Christ. Therefore, crisis or no crisis, Christians are to act as worshippers toward the God who sent us, and we are to seek to live as wise worshippers in light of future realities that are certainly due the promises of God.

---

11. Michael S. Northcott, "The Spirit of Environmentalism," in *The Care of Creation*, ed. R. J. Berry (Leicester, UK: InterVarsity, 2000), 168–69. We would be careful to point out that consuming natural resources is not the problem *per se*, but the inordinate pursuit of the "next new thing," as well as the overindulgence that often goes with it, is.

This is what Francis Bridger means when he says that Christian ethics "looks both back and forward. Yet even looking back is not to some kind of law code but to the decisive intervention of God in his Son who in his person represents the inauguration of the future kingdom."[12] It is both the worship mandate given in Genesis 1 and the call to a future hope that demands our proper treatment of the world God created us to be a part of and for us to live it. It is Christ's death and resurrection that make it possible. In other words, God desires that we live our lives as acts of worship that not only go out to evangelistically proclaim the reality of Christ but also to lead the entire created realm in maximizing the glory it returns to God by the way we live and move and have our being in our environment. We do this not only because it is right, but because it is good. Not just out of obedience, but in hopes of flourishing.

We see, then, that in regard to our ethics and our treatment of God's world, the coming of the kingdom of God does not overthrow the natural order but rather coincides with it, confirms it, and acts with care and reverence in anticipation of the beautiful transformation of it. As the late Princeton theology professor J. Christiaan Beker puts it, "The ethical activity of the Christian is motivated not only of Christ in the Spirit but also by the beckoning power of God's kingdom. And so God's past act in Christ and His future act in the resurrection of the dead converge on Christian life in the present."[13] Indeed, "Paul's apocalyptic faith in the transformation of the creation at the time of God's coming reign compels an ethic that strains and labours to move God's creation toward that future triumph of God promised in Jesus Christ and to which the presence of the Spirit propels us."[14]

The Shape of Christian Ethics: Conforming to Christ and Obeying His Commands

In fall 2002, the Evangelical Environmental Network organized and sponsored an educational campaign titled "What Would Jesus Drive? (WWJDrive)." The goal of the campaign was an attempt to get Christians to "discover new ways to love your neighbor as we strive together to

---

12. Francis Bridger, "Ecology and Eschatology: A Neglected Dimension," *Tyndale Bulletin* 41, no. 2 (1990): 295.
13. J. Christiaan Beker, *Paul's Apocalyptic Gospel: The Coming Triumph of God* (Philadelphia, PA: Fortress, 1982), 87.
14. Ibid., 111.

reduce fuel consumption and pollution from the cars, trucks, and SUVs we drive."[15] The website goes on to explain that,

> The question, "What Would Jesus Drive?" is a more specific version of the well-known question, "What Would Jesus Do?" Christians ask themselves "What Would Jesus Do?" to help guide them in their daily decisions as disciples (or followers) of Jesus Christ, who lives and reigns in their hearts. As followers, the question actually becomes, "Lord, what would you have me do?" So our specific question then becomes, "Lord, what would you have me drive?"[16]

What would Jesus do? Inherently, that question represents the moral and ethical quest of Christianity in both its simplest and most profound form. For on the one hand, if we could know and do what Jesus would do in each of our given situations, the moral life would be far simpler. Yet, discovering or determining what exactly Jesus would do in any given context and then learning how to develop the character and wherewithal to do it has been one of the most profound quests of human experience. To accomplish the task, some have sworn off sex, entered monasteries, and prayed 20 hours a day. Others have tattooed their entire bodies as a form of witness to the "down and out" of society. How does one go about determining what Jesus would do? How should knowing what Jesus would do actually influence what I should do?

Over the past century, the evangelical answer to these questions has largely come in the form of delineating biblical commands, rules, and principles of conduct that in turn spell out a Christian's duty in the language of do's and don'ts, rights and wrongs. Indeed, because the Scriptures are replete with commands and moral principles of behavior, one would be remiss to suggest that such an approach is wrongheaded. However, when exclusively emphasized or when not held in place with other important elements of ethics present in the New Testament—most notably gospel and mission—an emphasis on moral rule-making and keeping consistently ends up in legalism.

In Jesus' day it was the Pharisees who championed the ethics of moral duty and rule keeping largely devoid of an embedded sense of grace and mission. Their demanding code of moral religiosity earned them some of the harshest criticisms Jesus levied while sojourning on earth. In our day we must seriously consider if we are any better. Could it be that the

---

15. See http://www.whatwouldjesusdrive.info/intro.php. Accessed November 21, 2011.
16. Ibid.

form of ethics we have taught as conservative believers is little more than a rule-based "evangelical Phariseeism"?

Even among non-Christian ethicists, recent trends have been away from rule- and obligation-based systems of ethics. Consider, for example, the comments of Elizabeth Anscombe in her influential work "Modern Moral Philosophy." She writes, "The concepts of obligation, and duty—*moral* obligation and *moral* duty, that is to say—and of what is *morally* right and wrong, and of the *moral* sense of 'ought,' ought to be jettisoned if this is psychologically possible."[17] Indeed, for many years now, the assertion by Anscombe that deontic language should be done away with has been one of the dominant themes driving the revival in virtue theory.

Perhaps it is for this reason that in recent years there has been a trend in Christian ethics to "shift its focus much more toward virtues and the formation of character, and away from rules and principles."[18] That is, for the last several decades, there has been a growing movement in the world of ethics to shift from deontological ethics toward character or virtue ethics that are not just concerned with the question of *what we should do*, but *who we should be*. We are of the opinion that any presentation of an environmental ethic that makes a codification of moral rules and principles primary suffers from a deeper misunderstanding of the relationship of God to his creation and the inherent call within Scripture for all human beings to be the kind of people who display the character of one being conformed to the image of Christ.

On the other hand, while emphasizing a whole-person approach to ethics is a right and good corrective, unless the pursuit of virtue is both grounded in the nature of God, motivated by the grace of God, guided by the principles of his Word, and tied to the overall trajectory toward *True North*, it will eventually become nothing more than a rudderless ethical system following the winds of cultural preferences.[19] In the words of David Hume, such an ethic would be little more than a reflection of popular "sentimentality."

Fortunately, the Old and New Testament Scriptures give ample teaching for us to understand that there is a middle ground between these two extremes that serves as the best way for Christ's followers to converge on

17. Gertrude Elizabeth Margaret Anscombe, "Modern Moral Philosophy," *Philosophy* 33, no. 124 (1958), 1. Conversely, Christian ethicist Norman Geisler argues that Christian ethics is deontological and has no room for aretaic theory (*Christian Ethics*, 2nd ed. [Grand Rapids, MI: Baker Academic, 2010], 17–18).

18. Glenn Stassen and David Gushee, *Kingdom Ethics* (Downers Grove, IL: InterVarsity, 2003), 32.

19. An aretaic version, if you will, of Joseph Fletcher's "Christian" situation ethics.

an ethic of worship that takes seriously the mission of God. As Christopher Wright put it in his plenary address, the phrase "keeping the way of the Lord" connotes two possible pictures of how to live a life of faithfulness. On the one hand, "keeping the way of the Lord" implies a virtuous imitation of God; on the other hand, it implies "following the instructions that someone has given you to make sure you stay on the right path and do not wander off on wrong paths that may turn out to be dead ends or dangerous. . . . Obedience to the law of God and reflection of the character of God are not mutually exclusive categories: the one is an expression of the other."[20]

It is our conviction that in order for Christians to rightly live out the answer to the question What would Jesus do? we must hold together and understand the integrated nature of both the deontological and virtue aspects of ethics as they are revealed in Scripture. We would argue that there are four reasons why deontology and virtue ethics need each other in a scripturally driven environmental ethic.

The teaching of Scripture. First and foremost, the Scriptures indicate *both* virtues and absolute moral principles and commands are normative action guides for the people of God. To see this, consider the relationship between the *Shema* (Deut 6:4–5) and the Decalogue (Exodus 20). When God gave the Law to his people through Moses, he did so through both a command to be virtuous and specific action guides that spelled out what that virtue was supposed to look like. Israel was to "*love* the LORD" their God with all their heart, soul, and might. The Decalogue indicated specific commands that when followed would demonstrate what loving God with heart and soul was supposed to actually look like in practice. The command to be a God lover (virtue) is followed up with a series of more particular commands related to actions (deontology). Deuteronomy 10:12–14 clearly indicates the co-dependent relationship between virtue and deontology:

---

20. Christopher Wright, "The Obedience of Faith Among the Nations: Old Testament Ethics in Covenantal and Missional Perspective," a plenary paper presented at the Evangelical Theological Society, November 14, 2007, 5–6. Even within non-Christian ethical methodologies, there has recently been a new turn in virtue ethics, which has realized the important connection between virtue and deontology. For further exploration, see Jesse Couenhoven, "Against Metaethical Imperialism: Several Arguments for Equal Partnerships between the Deontic and Aretaic," *Journal of Religious Ethics* 38, no. 3 (2010): 521–44. See also Frans Svensson, "Virtue Ethics and the Search for an Account of Right Action," *Ethical Theory and Moral Practice* 13 (2010): 255–71. Finally, Stanley Hauerwas and Charles Pinches (*Christians Among the Virtues* [Notre Dame, IN: University of Notre Dame Press, 1997], 57–61) argue that there have been a number of ethicists who have attempted to address this relationship. For instance, Philippa Foot has argued for supererogatory morality, William Frankena has attempted to associate virtue with the moral subject in order to stress the importance of the subject, and Edmund Pincoff introduces the mandatory virtues.

> Now, Israel, what does the LORD your God require from you, but to fear the LORD your God, to walk in all His ways and *love* Him, and to serve the LORD your God with all your heart and with all your soul, and to keep the LORD's *commandments* and His *statutes* which I am commanding you today for your good? Behold, to the LORD your God belong heaven and the highest heavens, the earth and all that is in it (emphasis mine).

Second, consider the teachings in the Sermon on the Mount (Matthew 5–7). Here Jesus draws a distinction between what appears to be moral behavior—the moralism of the Pharisees—and the proper worshipful obedience of a disciple. Jesus "made a distinction between the law of Moses and the rabbinic interpretations of it, which had come to have the form of unwritten law. He often challenged these interpretations, pointing out how ridiculous some of them were."[21] Thus, in the Sermon on the Mount, far from removing absolute standards of action and conduct in favor of a virtuous disposition before God, Jesus actually reaffirmed the absolute norms of Scripture and then gave them proper application. One particular case in which he did this pertains to his instruction regarding adultery. In Matt 5:27–28, Jesus states, "You have heard that it was said, 'You shall not commit adultery;' but I say to you that everyone who looks at a woman with lust for her has already committed adultery with her in his heart." Not only is the virtue of faithfulness assumed as the right character trait, but Jesus goes on to reassert the norm of the command not to commit adultery and even specifies a higher standard of what breaking that command entails: do not even look at a woman lustfully.

Deontology, then, plays a vitally important role for the believer to understand *how* to love God. Very specifically, Jesus asserts that he did not come to nullify the law but to fulfill it. And in order to fulfill the law, Jesus' disciples would need not only to have good intentions and a loving heart, they would need to demonstrate their love via particular forms of behavior as indicated by the moral commands of Scripture. As we see in this brief example, Jesus indicates that the particular principles of conduct remain in force. As Scott Rae puts it, "In the Sermon on the Mount (Matthew 5–7), [Jesus] does not nullify the Law. Rather he critiques the Pharisees for their misinterpretation and misapplication of it. He deepens the requirements of the Law and promotes to both the religious leaders and general population a deontology that is both action and

---

21. Roger H. Crook, *An Introduction to Christian Ethics*, 2nd ed. (Englewood Cliffs, NJ: Prentice Hall, 1995), 68.

intent oriented."[22] Thus, as the Scripture indicates, the blessed life—the life of flourishing as a disciple of Jesus Christ—involves a moral center that focuses on both virtue and command. Indeed, as Jesus indicates in John 14:15 and 21, respectively, "If you love Me, you will keep My commandments," and "He who has My commandments and keeps them is the one who loves Me." According to Jesus, both the virtues of character and particular obedience to commands are necessities in the moral development of the people of God.

Virtues receive their content from behavior commands. The second reason we must understand why deontological and virtue theories need each other is that throughout the Scriptures, virtues function primarily as *formal categories* that describe the intent or quality of good moral character, not primarily as specified action guides related to the inherent quality of the act chosen or performed. That is, virtues are meant to describe the *quality* of the person and indicate what ought to be the character and motive of the person. They do not, however, describe the *material content* of the behavior in the sense they do not function as "principles of conduct" but "principles of character." For this reason, when dealing with concrete situations, the only way to avoid virtues devolving into well-intended relativism is to guide them with action principles that are themselves normative absolutes.

The virtues of love and wisdom become the key words knowingly or unknowingly camouflaging a reason-based analysis of circumstances and situations that in turn indicate how one ought to adjust one's understanding of the application of commands in particular scenarios. Howard Marshall captures the essence of this point on why virtues need deontology when he critiques a perspective that claims "the principle of love" as the chief action guide to the Christian life. He writes, "Some modern interpreters seem to reduce the list [of normative commands] to the one principle of love. Thereby they may fail in practice to recognize that not all love is rightly inspired and conducted, and that true love must be governed by principle."[23] Thomas Aquinas was right when he concluded that it is not just the virtue of love or practical wisdom that is needed for moral rectitude but *rightly* ordered love and *right* practical reason.[24] We believe that this is also the basic point John Calvin was making when he

---

22. Scott Rae, *Moral Choices* (Grand Rapids, MI: Zondervan, 2000), 28.

23. I. Howard Marshall, *Beyond the Bible: Moving from Scripture to Theology* (Grand Rapids, MI: Baker, 2004), 40.

24. Thomas Aquinas, *Summa Theologica* I–II.91.4, I–II.92.1 reply 1; I–II.95.1.

indicated that there is a third use of the Law that is meant to guide the believer into the proper material form of living and worship.[25]

In sum, principles of character need to be informed by principles of conduct. Scripture and scripturally identified absolute principles, norms, and rules are what inform rightly ordered virtues and which enable the task of Christian ethics. Scriptural principles and norms are not meant to be in conflict with love or the Holy Spirit's guidance—they are meant to shape and guide our understanding of it. When the call to love is left without clear action principles to tell us how to love, what might appear to be a solid ethical foundation (neighbor love) can quickly devolve into little more than culturally conditioned self-perceptions.[26]

Thus, an ethic that recognizes that virtuous qualities need action principles, commands, norms, and rules for guidance is not only holistic in nature but on the applied level is also more helpful than patting someone on the back and saying "Love God and rely on the Holy Spirit." This is particularly true when the help that someone asks for in a given circumstance may not be self-evident or when the person involved is confused by emotion or lack of moral grounding.

Norms of behavior find proper expression in a person of virtue. The third reason deontology and virtues need each other can be discovered when evaluating what lies at the heart of Jesus' critique of Phariseeism. Consider the stinging criticism Jesus makes of the Pharisaical system of morality in Matt 23:25–28:

> Woe to you, scribes and Pharisees, hypocrites! For you clean the outside of the cup and of the dish, but inside they are full of robbery and self-indulgence. You blind Pharisee, first clean the inside of the cup and of the dish, so that the outside of it may become clean also. Woe to you, scribes and Pharisees, hypocrites! For you are like whitewashed tombs, which on the outside appear beautiful, but inside they are full of dead men's bones and all uncleanness. So you, too, outwardly appear righteous to men, but inwardly you are full of hypocrisy and lawlessness.

---

25. John Calvin, *The Institutes of the Christian Religion*, I.12.3; 2.2.18; III.6.2.

26. Ray S. Anderson, *An Emergent Theology for Emerging Churches* (Downers Grove, IL: InterVarsity, 2006), 147. Perhaps the clearest and most current example of the possible ambiguity that results when an ethic championing what is good is pitted against what is right is the ambiguity present within certain branches of the "Emerging Church Movement" regarding the issue of homosexuality. What does neighbor love look like for a person who claims to have a clear and enduring "psycho-sexual orientation" towards members of his or her own sex? Certainly we are called to love him or her as neighbor, but what does that love look like and how might biblical passages like Romans 1 and 1 Cor 6:9 guide the answer? Ironically, Anderson's own system makes him a purveyor of these "culturally conditioned self-perceptions" that he specifically states he desires to avoid.

Even though these men were masters of keeping what they interpreted to be even the minutest elements of the law, Jesus was unimpressed. In fact, in Jesus' eyes, the epitome of hypocrisy is the performance of principles, rules, and norms of behavior without a love for God that drives them. As Christopher Wright pointed out in his aforementioned plenary address, ethics for the people of God is never to be a means of gaining God's redemption, "but as a response to God's redeeming grace. Any other foundation leads to pride, legalism, or despair."[27] Therefore, while it is right to hold that rules, norms, and commands give material substance to the virtues, having and being virtuous is the crucial element of morality that rescue rules, norms, and commands from cold legalism and performance-based religiosity. For the people of God, it is a love that results from a grace received and is motivated to spread that good news that must be the engine for the moral life. To this point, Jesus was clear. The quality of moral behavior and the right ordering of actions that conform to an outward standard depends on the inward orientation of heart. While a tree is known by its fruits, there is no question that the type of fruits produced depends on the roots and kind of tree it is.

What do we mean by saying that "having and being virtuous is crucial to rescue morality from cold legalism?" We mean that right actions must be motivated by a love of God in order for them to have ultimate worth. Much more than desiring disciples that merely mimicked moral patterns of behavior, Jesus

> Wanted to bring people into a relationship with God that would reshape their character. He assumed that the kind of person one is determines the kind of thing one does. For him, the crucial point is "Either make the tree good and its fruit good, or make the tree bad, and its fruit bad; for the tree is known by its fruit" (Matthew 12:33). . . . While he did not assume that a good person automatically does good things, he did assume that character determines conduct.[28]

Scott Rae is correct to point out that along with a deontological element, Christian ethics must have a substantial place in it for an ethic of virtue "since a major part of the Christian moral life involves emulating the character traits of Christ and exemplifying the fruit of the Spirit."[29] But going further than Rae, the deontological nature of Christian ethics

---

27. Wright, "The Obedience of Faith," 13.
28. Crook, *An Introduction to Christian Ethics*, 71.
29. Rae, *Moral Choices*, 17.

needs to be *at least* balanced with the emphasis on virtue and, in our opinion, even subordinated to and centrally oriented toward the pursuit of Christlike character and the command to love God by becoming a virtuous person. Jesus said, that the greatest commandment is to *love* God with all one's heart, soul, mind, and strength and to *love* one's neighbor as oneself (see Mark 12:29–31).

Metaphorically speaking, the danger with a pure or dominant deontology is that it places the discipline of ethics at great risk of losing its heart. That is, when one focuses on deontology and reduces the moral project to mere absolutism *alone*, the discipline of ethics that is meant to be a worshipful and joyous pursuit of God becomes much like Dorothy's "Tin Man" who has no heart, only the echo of morality in his breast, and is ever in danger of rusting into rigidity with the threatening ax of moralism in hand.

The symbiotic loop of deontology and virtue. Finally, the fourth reason deontology and virtues need each other has to do with the symbiotic nature (or mutually reinforcing relationship) that exists between deontology and virtue ethics. Paul Ramsey pointed this out in his classic *Basic Christian Ethics*, when he argued that Christian ethics should be understood as "obedient love."[30] Crook explains this idea well when he states,

> The central imperative in Christian ethics is summed up in the term *obedient love*. The word *obedient* ties Christian morality to the idea of the sovereignty of God. . . . It associates the concepts of justice, right, duty, value, virtue, and calling to one's relationship to God. It gives an objective reference to the Christian life by suggesting that its requirements are established by God, not by human decision. It says, in short, that what is right, just, valuable, and good are **discovered** by human beings rather than **determined** by them.[31]

Either a deontological methodology or virtue methodology employed without the other robs Christian ethics of its depth and coherence. Principles, commands, rules, and duties need to be understood in terms of shaping one's disposition to love and worship God rightly in order to avoid devolution into an anemic Pharisaical legalism. Virtues need the directing guidance of principles, rules, and norms to keep them from devolving into culturally relative personality preferences.

---

30. Paul Ramsey, *Basic Christian Ethics* (New York: Charles Scribner's Sons, 1951), xi.

31. Crook, *An Introduction to Ethics*, 68–69; emphasis added. Interestingly enough, Crook does not go on to develop the link of obedience to norms of behavior or commands as much as he does to general virtues. His insightful quote here is left somewhat empty in content because of this.

The beautiful thing about this both/and perspective is that it is not only rooted in the orthodox biblical tradition handed down from the Israelites to the church fathers, it also has a certain symbiotic energy that compels it.[32] One of the most beautiful elements of this relationship between deontology and virtue is the symbiotic nature that results as both action commands and virtue development are pursued in light of each other. To see this, consider once again the teaching of Jesus in John 14:15 and 21, respectively: "If you love Me, you will keep My commandments," and "He who has My commandments and keeps them is the one who loves Me."

Commands and principles demonstrate the proper form of action and obedience (John 14:15). Repeated obedience, in turn, leads to habits of practice. Eventually these habits of practice will become habits of the heart or virtues. These virtues in turn will form the basic building blocks of godly character. People who have godly character love to obey the commands of Jesus (John 14:21).

What emerges, then, can best be described as a "deontological virtue ethic" where deontology is the adjective to describe how to rightly order virtues both to the proper ultimate goal (loving God) and in proper expression in particular circumstances. Rightly understood, the commands of Scripture should not be relegated to prima facie principles that are relevant only in light of virtuous motivations and intentions; rather, they are given by God to instruct, guard, and guide virtues. They champion the cause of virtues by keeping them from falling prey to the ever-changing winds of cultural and societal sentiments.

On the other hand, the absolute commands of God are not ends in themselves. One does not obey merely for obedience sake. Rather, when properly understood, ethics flows out of the created order and seeks to return unto God the glory he is due. A truly Christian perspective on ethics understands that the action commands of God are meant to be a means to the end of rightly ordered worship expressed ethically in the lives of God's people who are virtuous in character because they are obediently striving to be like Jesus. It is through a deontological virtue ethic, then, that the Christian life enters the self-feeding loop of obeying God to demonstrate love for him and loving him by obeying him as John 14:15 and 21 instruct.

---

32. Consider both Augustine and Aquinas as great examples of men who developed systems of virtue while simultaneously understanding and affirming that absolute nature of God's moral action commands. Aquinas, in particular, developed a system that championed virtues but also indicated the importance of understanding law (with particular regard to natural law) as crucial to guiding morality to its proper end.

As we have clearly stated, this is a project designed to locate the discussion of Christian environmental ethics in the person of Jesus Christ. Therefore, we have painstakingly and intentionally elevated the question of *who* above the related question of *how* in an effort to properly orient ourselves towards a position of *True North*. The purpose of this section, then, has been to demonstrate that any subsequently derived principles for environmental ethics must follow the example of Christ. That is to say, Christians should utilize deontology to rightly order their proper love for God and his creation towards his greater glory.

IV. Conclusion

Finally now, as we bring our pursuit of *True North* to a conclusion, we have ultimately come to discover the most important truth in the universe. That is, both the creation and new creation are brought together and find their ultimate culmination in Christ. He is the unifying principle who gives both coherence and continuity to all things.[33] We have learned that "the true humanity of Jesus is the climax of the history of creation and at the same time the starting point of the new creation."[34]

Through our study of key passages like Genesis 1–3, Colossians 1, Romans 8, 2 Peter 3, and Revelation 21–22, we have also uncovered two other crucial realities related to our larger discussion of environmental ethics and creation care. First, God created the universe through the agency of the Second Person of the Trinity with an inherent *exitus et reditus* pattern by which all things are created by God and for God to bring glory unto God. Second, they also demonstrate a weighty affirmation of the material order that is Christologically underwritten in the creation, incarnation, resurrection, and second coming.[35]

The former of these realities places a structural framework around our ethical thinking that demands of us a consideration of every moment of our lives mattering before God. Indeed, not only is this true for us but it is also true for all humans who have ever lived as well as for the existence of all aspects of the created realm. God created all of it for His own glory. Thus how we live in it, treat it, use it, care for it, direct it, are all reflective of our view of God and our view of what belongs to him.

---

33. Bridger, "Ecology and Eschatology," 298.
34. N. T. Wright, *Colossians and Philemon* (Leicester, UK: InterVarsity; Grand Rapids, MI: Eerdmans, 1986), 70.
35. Bridger, "Ecology and Eschatology," 300.

The latter of these realities tells us that no matter what else we do or think, we cannot be excused for treating the created order as if it does not matter to God. The consistent pattern of affirmation of the created matter and order throughout the Scripture demands of us that we both recognize and live as if God loves the world he created and he cares greatly about what happens to it.

Thus we can affirm that while the new creation is the beginning of a cosmic renewal of all things, it is also to be an ethical transformation. Our transformation by the grace of God is only the beginning of a new heavens and a new earth (Isa 65:17–18; 66:22; 2 Pet 3:10–13; Rev 21:1–4) and a new way to perceive life itself. Further, John Frame states, "Believers are the beginning of a work of Christ, by which he will eventually reconcile 'all things' to himself (Col 1:15–20)."[36] The gospel, then, functions to complete the purpose of the original creation by providing the basis for the transformation and ultimately the consummation of all things. Frame goes on to write, "we may perhaps even say that the new creation completes the old, even though in the end that completion will be a drastic reconstruction (2 Pet 3:12; cf. 1 Cor 3:12–15)."[37]

Now and Not Yet

Now as we live in this world that has been redeemed but not yet fully transformed . . . as we live between now and the Day of the Lord when all things are renewed, Scripture tells us we live in a period of waiting that theologians call "now and not yet." Ken Keathley explains:

> The Bible presents the "now—not yet" experience of being between the beginning and completion of salvation as a tension that is often called inaugurated eschatology. When Scripture speaks of the work of Christ or the believer's position in him, salvation is presented as an objective, finished reality (Eph 1:3). But when the Bible deals with the believer's daily walk and practical living, redemption is characterized as a subjective, ongoing work (Phil 2:13). It is important to distinguish between these two conceptions. The believer now enjoys all the objective blessings of salvation, but he is yet to realize the full redemption—the

---

36. John Frame, *The Doctrine of God* (Phillipsburg, NJ: P&R, 2002), 297.
37. Ibid.

glorification—of his body. This tension is lived out as a practical matter in the lifelong sanctifying walk of faith.[38]

In this place of "tension," humans are called to live a life of responsible worship in all that we do. We are each called to live responsibly before God as individuals, and we are all responsible for how we treat and care for his creation.

This is why Bruce Little is right when he says, "What is really needed is an active moral compass within each individual [and the Church united] encouraging the responsible use of creation. Man is not called only to care for creation as he finds it; he is also to be a good steward as he develops, investigates, enjoys, and enlarges creation (creative stewardship)."[39] In order to do this, his compass must be clearly set to *True North*. He goes on to point out that "here again, man is always to realize creative stewardship must be done with an acute awareness that creation ultimately belongs to God. This view of creation should shape the assumptions held about what is permissible as creative stewardship is exercised."[40]

This creative stewardship is not always easy. Indeed, this life of ours is a journey where we encounter the echoes of joy that God allows to linger in the air of an environment filled with the adversity of the world, the flesh, and the devil; where stunning acts of kindness are matched step for step and exceeded by the horrors of war, crime, and selfishness; where great triumphs are tasted but only in the midst of great sorrows and regrets. We live in a world of amazing beauty, yet one also marred by trash, decay, death.

Conclusion: Maranatha

It will not always be this way. The good news of the Bible—indeed the culminating news of the grand narrative of creation, fall, redemption, and restoration—is that some day the "not yet" will indeed become the "now." When that day comes, the promises of Scripture are stunning and can be described in the following way:

- The created order will be found and transformed into its purest and most wonderful form.

---

38. Kenneth Keathley, "The Work of God: Salvation," in *A Theology for the Church*, ed. Danny Akin (Nashville, TN: B&H, 2007), 696.

39. Bruce Little, "Creation and Creative Stewardship Responsibility," *TheoEcology* 1 (January 2012): 7–8.

40. Ibid.

- The people of God will have their bodies totally renewed and transformed.
- The dead who have gone before us in Christ will meet us and dine with us in sweet and tender reunion.
- "Diversity is not destroyed in eternity but cleansed from sin and made serviceable to fellowship with God and others."[41]
- The sicknesses and sorrows and disappointments of this broken and vain world will be no more.
- We will experience the freedom from all temptation, for the source of all temptation will be completely conquered at last.
- Every tear—every single one of them—for all the regrets and losses and sins and hurts will be wiped away.
- Mourning will turn into dancing.
- Night will be replaced by everlasting light.
- Streets will be made of gold, and living water will flow clean, sparkling, and melodious through the city of God.
- God's people will taste the fruit of the once forbidden tree of life.
- And then—surpassing all wonders and joys—the redeemed in Christ will look and see that the One whom they have most longed to meet and know and love and be loved by is there among them.
- And the new creation is filled with the knowledge of the Lord's glory as the waters cover the sea (Isa 11:9; Hab 2:14)!

So, as it was meant to be in the beginning, so it ever shall be. Christ will reign supreme over creation from beginning to end. Under his rule, the new creation and its transformed inhabitants will forever find fullness of joy. He is the Alpha and Omega, the Author and Finisher of our Faith. It is in this reality that finding and pursuing *True North* takes on so much potency for the life here in the "now and not yet." Puritan Thomas Chalmers eloquently captured this idea in his timeless work *The Expulsive Power of a New Affection*. He writes,

> There are two ways in which a practical moralist may attempt to displace from the human heart its love of the world—either by a demonstration of the world's vanity, so that the heart shall be prevailed upon simply to withdraw its regards from an object that is not worthy of it; or, by setting forth another object, even God, as more worthy of its attachment, so that the heart shall be prevailed upon not to resign an

---

41. Herman Bavinck, *Reformed Dogmatics: Holy Spirit, Church, and New Creation*, vol. 4, ed. John Bolt, trans. John Vriend (Grand Rapids, MI: Baker, 2008), 715.

old affection, which shall have nothing to succeed it, but to exchange
an old affection for a new one.[42]

Oh, that our affections would be fully riveted on Christ! That we might
long for this as we taste of the kindness of our God (1 Pet 2:3) in creating
us, redeeming us, and promising this kind of transformation of the entire
cosmos! This is what Paul speaks of in Romans 8 when he acknowledges
the groaning of creation. Bullmore captures it well with the following
observation:

> The images Paul uses to speak of this future redemption are powerfully
> emotive: the removal of an absolutely frustrating encumbrance, libera-
> tion from a killing servitude, the successful completion of a seemingly
> endless travail. But it is in his phrase "glorious freedom" (v. 21) that
> Paul strikes the most potent chord, for here he speaks of the return of
> creation to a state in which it can once again freely and perfectly fulfill
> God's purpose for it and by so doing participate in the general glory
> which will one day be revealed, not only in us, but as the controlling
> characteristic of Christ's eternal kingdom.[43]

It will be on that day that perhaps the greatest gift the Lord can give us
in his presence will be the joyful rest or Sabbath that can only come with
total fulfillment and the removal of all opposing forces that exist in this
present darkness. Rest will be ours. Not merely the cessation of activities,
but the experience of reaching a goal of crucial importance. Rest that
comes only at "the completion of the Christian's pilgrimage, [at] the end
of the struggle against the flesh, the world, and the devil."[44]

It will be at that time that all will realize that the moral and spiritual
compass that points to *True North* does not point to the restored creation. Rather, it points a restored creation to the source and fulfillment
of its being and longing. It points a restored creation to the One in whom
it finds its fullest flourishing. For it is in the presence of God, a presence
whose sheer beauty is always drawing us onward, that we find strength
for the journey. It is in seeing Christ Jesus face to face that every eye and
every heart will be ever freshly filled with the wonder of the One who has

42. Thomas Chalmers, "The Expulsive Power of a New Affection," in *The Works of Thomas Chalmers* (New York: Robert Carter, 1830). Volume 2 is also found in *The Protestant Pulpit*, ed. Andrew Watterson Blackwood (Grand Rapids, MI: Baker, 1947), 50.

43. Michael A. Bullmore, "The Four Most Important Biblical Passages for a Christian Environmentalism," *Trinity Journal* 19 (1998): 161.

44. Millard Erickson, *Christian Theology* (Grand Rapids, MI: Baker, 1983), 1229–30.

removed the curse and wiped away every tear. It is in that final "welcome home my child, well done!" that the consummation of all things created is found.

God himself is the end of the long, hard march. He is the one safe home after a rough journey in a fallen land. He, and he alone, is the hope of eternity. Jesus Christ is the Creator who made us to worship him, the Redeemer who rescued us to worship him, and the Returning King who restores us and all the cosmos so that we can worship him in an ever-expanding joy as we ought to forever and ever and ever.

> In Your presence is fullness of joy
> In Your right hand there are pleasures forever. (Ps 16:11b)

Maranatha, come Lord Jesus.

Name Index

Gunton, Colin E.   *89, 91, 94–95, 103, 137*
Gushee, David   *146*

H

Hammett, John   *56*
Hargrove, Eugene   *12, 15*
Harrelson, Walter   *38*
Hauerwas, Stanley   *147*
Hessel, Dieter   *12*
Heumann, Joseph K.   *13*
Hodge, Charles   *131, 141*
Hunter, James Davidson   *10, 19, 135*

I

Irenaeus   *94–95*

J

Jamieson, Robert   *62*
Jeffery, Steve   *88, 90*

K

Keathley, Kenneth   *108, 155–56*
Kline, Meredith G.   *62*
Kreeft, Peter   *45*

L

Leopold, Aldo   *14*
Lewis, C. S.   *49, 118–19*
Lewis, Gordon   *99–101*
Liederbach, Mark   *8, 19, 24, 27, 46, 121*
Light, Andrew   *11–12*
Little, Bruce   *20, 156*
Lovelock, James   *116–17*
Luther, Martin   *46–47*

M

MacArthur, John   *112, 119, 121*
Mahaney, C. J.   *96*
Manahan, Ronald   *69, 77*

Marshall, I. Howard   *149*
May, William E.   *48*
McDaniel, Donald R., Jr.   *16–17*
McGrath, Alister   *30, 36–37, 39, 42, 44, 50, 67, 92*
McNeill, John T.   *47*
Meilaender, Gilbert   *74*
Moo, Douglas J.   *88, 93–94, 99*
Moore, Louis A.   *107, 109, 125–27, 133*
Moreland, J. P.   *75*
Murray, John   *65–66*
Murray, Robin L.   *13*

N

Nash, James A.   *70–71, 73*
Nelson, David P.   *34*
Northcott, Michael S.   *16, 73, 79, 105, 142–43*

O

O'Donovan, O. M. T.   *97–98, 132, 135*
Ovey, Michael   *88, 90*

P

Packer, J. I.   *55, 64–65, 75, 88–89, 96, 129*
Patterson, Paige   *130–31*
Phillips, J. B.   *142*
Pinches, Charles   *147*
Pincoff, Edmund   *147*
Poythress, Vern S.   *71, 78*

R

Rae, Scott B.   *75, 148–49, 151*
Ramsey, Paul   *152*
Rasmussen, Larry   *12*
Reid, Alvin   *8, 19, 24, 27, 121*
Rodgers, Adrian   *83, 97*
Rolston, Holmes, III   *11–12, 14–15*
Rust, Eric   *16*

Subject Index

165

Scripture Index